India

Through The Ages

A Survey of The Growth of
Indian Life and Thought

Sir
Jadunath
Sarkar

SANAGE
PUBLISHING HOUSE

Paperback: 978-936205782-2
Hardback: 978-936205105-9
eBook: 978-936205297-1

Printed by:

Sanage Publishing House LLP
Mumbai, India

sanagepublishing@gmail.com

Sir Jadunath Sarkar, CIE, FRAS (10 December 1870 – 19 May 1958) was a prominent Indian historian and a specialist on the Mughal dynasty. Sarkar was educated in English literature, worked as a teacher for some period of time but later shifted his focus to history research writing. He had vast knowledge of Persian language and all his books he wrote in English.

PEEFACE

This book contains the first course of Sir William Meyer lectures delivered by me at the Madras University in March 1928, with Sir Venkataratnam Naidu, Vice Chancellor, in the chair. A survey of India's growth through the ages, when confined within the limits of a course of six lectures, is bound to consist of generalizations and to give only the broad features of the country's development. Minute illustrations and justificative evidence cannot be supplied but the very lack of these deprives the author of the means of meeting possible objections in advance. References to sources have been given in the footnotes in important points only. Then, again, certain passages in these lectures have no pretension to originality, as the lines of thought and reasoning followed by me therein had been first marked out by some preceding writers, and my work has consisted in continuing what they began, in supplying useful details and in weaving their thoughts into the texture of my survey. This is specially the case in the chapter on Buddhism and its history in India. In certain other passages I have repeated what I had previously written on the same subjects such as Islam's work in India and the Indian Renaissance in the 19th century. This was necessary in order to give completeness to the survey.

It will be noticed that this study of India's past practically confines itself to Northern India and that all the illustrations of the British period are taken from Bengal and Bengali literature. This restriction has not sprung from, any narrow spirit of provincialism nor any contempt for the glorious past of the Southern land, but is the result of the necessities of the case. My survey would have consisted of hazy and commonplace generalizations only, if I had extended it over the entire Indian continent, instead of confining my gaze to a homogeneous and compact group of facts relating to one province. The objective basis of these discourses had to be made firm and to be built up from facts known to me from original study. If I had tried to import details drawn from Southern India, I should have gone out of the depths of my personal knowledge and presented second-hand information; nor could I have succeeded in fitting a few South Indian examples into the body of my illustrations which are all taken from Northern India. My subject would then most probably have lost the organic connection of its parts.

Though the limitations of my knowledge and the needs of the case have prevented me from doing justice to the contributions of Madras and Mysore to the evolution of modern India, it is to be hoped that some South Indian scholar will work out the cultural history of our country from the point of view of local knowledge, on the lines sketched by me in the following pages from the Northern angle of vision.

JADUNATH SARKAR

Contents

I

THE ARYANS AND THEIR LEGACY TO INDIA

We usually study the history of India as divided into watertight compartments or periods. One great defect of this method of treatment is that we thereby lose sight of the life of the nation as a whole, we fail to realize that India has been the home of a living growing people, with a continuity running through all the ages, each generation using, expanding, or modifying what its long line of predecessors had left to it.

The Indian people form one common and distinct type.

No careful student of our history can help being struck by one supreme characteristic of the Indian people. It is their vitality as a distinct type, with a distinct civilization of their own and a mind as active after centuries of foreign rule as ever in the past. The Indian people of today are no doubt a composite ethnical product but whatever their different constituent elements may have been in origin, they have all acquired a common Indian stamp, and have all been contributing to a common culture and building up a common type of traditions, thought and literature. Even Sir Herbert Eisley, who is so sceptical about the Indians' claim to be considered as one people, has been forced to admit that "Beneath the manifold diversity of physical and social type, language, custom and religion, which strikes the observer in India, there can still be discerned a certain 'underlying uniformity of life from the Himalayas to Cape Comorin.' There is in fact an Indian character, a general Indian personality, which we cannot resolve into its component elements." {People of India, 2nd ed., p. 299).

This common Indian type has stood the test of time, it has outlived the shock of dynastic revolutions, foreign invasions, religious conflicts, and widespread natural disasters. Its best right to live is the vital power displayed by it. through many thousand years of cataclysmic change in our land.

The historic makers of modern India.

Each race or creed that has chosen India for its home, each dynasty that has enjoyed settled rule among us for some time, each school of thought that has dominated the human mind even in a single province of India,—has left its gifts which have worked in all the provinces and through many centuries, till they have lost their identity by being transformed and assimilated into the common store of India's legacy from the forgotten past,—Just as millions and millions of small coral insects through countless ages have given up their bodies in building up the reefs on which many of the Pacific islands now stand secure from the rage of the fiercest tempest.

It is the duty of the historian not to let that past be forgotten. He must trace these gifts back to their sources, give them their due places in the time-scheme, and show how they influenced or prepared the succeeding ages, and what portion of present-day Indian life and thought is the distinctive contribution of each race or creed that has lived in this land.

Such an analysis, in the present state of our knowledge, cannot be expected to be mathematically accurate or documented in every detail. It requires the highest historical imagination to reconstruct our past in this light, and, where imagination is the motive force, individual differences of opinion must occur. We cannot altogether eliminate the personal factor in such cases. But the attempt has to be made, if we are ever to rise above the level of our school text-books of Indian history. And, in spite of the risks attending a first attempt in a new field and the limited time at my disposal, I propose, in the present series of lectures, to make a survey of India's inner life and outer growth from the standpoint of evolutionary development through the ages.

How India's geography has influenced her history.

In India, as in every other country of the world, the geographical factor has profoundly influenced history. India is a continent, rather than one country, in respect of the diversity of the physical conditions of its different provinces. Leaving the Himalayan slopes and secluded valleys out of our account, we have Aryavarta, i.e., Hindustan proper or North India, forming one boundless plain with an assured water supply, which permits cavalry hordes to sweep from one end of it to the other in the dry season that begins in October. Hence, North India has been the seat of vast empires, each of which has, in its day, ruled over many provinces, maintained rich and learned Courts, and added to the common culture of all India. The Madras coast (popularly called the Eastern Karnatak) has the same features, though in a narrower area. But the Deccan proper, or the tableland of the south, is cut up by nature into small isolated districts, where racial and linguistic differences have been preserved through ages with very little change. And, hence, the history of the Deccan proper has been a record of the rise of numberless petty kingdoms, their eternal contest with their neighbours, and downfall one after another. Unlike Hindustan, this region of the South has failed to exert any influence on the other parts of India, but has succumbed to Hindustan or the Karnatak whenever its geographical isolation has been broken by the aggression of some great empire of those parts.

Immigrant rates in India.

The mainstream of immigration into India has come through the north-western passes. It is true, that at the other extremity or the north-eastern, frontier, there are some routes leading into India from Upper Burma and from Arrakan. But the heavy rainfall of this region, exceeding a hundred inches in the year concentrated into four months, soon washes away the tracks and promotes a dense growth of trees and underwood which closes the routes altogether in a few years. Moreover, Central Asia, the cradle-land of mankind for many ages, is near our n.-w. passages, while China, — another home of a teeming and overflowing population, —is cut off from the n.-e. corner of Assam by almost insuperable natural obstacles. The few foreign strains that are known to have entered India through the north-eastern passes were small in numerical strength. They were (i) a Tibetan dynasty that established a short-lived kingship in North Bengal in the 10th century,* (ii) the Ahoms who crossed the Patkoi range into the valley of the Brahmaputra early in the 13th century and fell completely under Hindu influence in the course of the next three centuries, and (iii) the Burmese who invaded Assam in 1816, only to be expelled by the English nine years later.

* Bangarli (Dinajpur) pillar inscription, 966 A.D.,— "Kambojānvayena gaudapatina"

The Mongolian settlement in Eastern Bengal is now an entirely lost chapter of Indian history but it must have been spread over several centuries and seems to have adopted the land and sea routes alike. Not only have the north-western passes poured forth teeming thousands into India ever since the dawn of history, but our western sea-board has been equally hospitable to immigrants. Phoenicians of the Biblical times, then Arabs, then Greeks and Alexandrian Romans, Persians, Abyssinians, and other foreigners have traded* with the western ports of India and made settlements on this coast. We know that Greek mercenary soldiers were engaged by some Hindu kings in historic times, as French adventurers were employed by Sindhia and the Nizam in the eighteenth century.

At the end of the middle-ages, our undefended western seaboard was penetrated by the Portuguese, and later by the Dutch, the English, and the French but the foreign settlements on our west coast were of an even earlier origin, as the Portuguese on their arrival (1498) found the Arabs already settled at the ports of Malabar.

We know that the first body of Parsis migrated from Iran to the Bombay coast about 735 A. D. The Chitpavan and Nagar Brahmans are two other immigrant foreign clans if their traditions and inscriptions can be relied upon to lift the veil from their racial origins. An analysis of the population of Gujrat shows many foreign races settled there but now completely Indianized. The Navaiyat Arabs and the Ben-i-Israel of Konkan are two other examples of this class, besides the Abyssinians of Janjira and the Nestorian Christians of Malabar.

---

* This trade pursued the route round Cape Comorin and up the east coast to the mouths of the Kaveri and the Krishna. Huge hoards of gold coins of the early. Roman empire has been dug out at the old mouths of the rivers in this part of the Madras Presidency. (See Periplus of the Erythræan Sea, a Greek work written about 78 A.D.). The Arab settlement on our Malabar coast is described in the Arabic work, *Zain-ud-din's Tuhafat-ul-Mujahidin* which has been translated into English (1833) by Rowlandson and into Portuguese by Prof. David Lopes (A Historia dos *Portugueses no Malabar* por Zinadin).

But, on our east coast, the ancient Indians were more enterprising and more skilled in navigation; they were colonizers, traders, givers of civilization to foreign lands, and not passive receivers. In historic times the Chola fleet dominated the Bay of Bengal, and Rajendra Chola I (*circa 1026* A.D.) captured the capital of Pegu (Lower Burma) and annexed the Andaman and Nicobar Islands. Indian emigrants, —mostly from the Pallava country, with several also from the Gangetic valley in the north, —colonized Sumatra, Java, Bali, Borneo, Cambodia, and Siam and gave a new religion, civilization, and art to the natives, though they did not establish political dominion there. The Indian mariners of the east coast, —whether from Tamluk in Bengal or Masulipatam in Madras, — disputed the monopoly of the trade in the Bay of Bengal and the eastern seas with the Chinese sailors, as readers of the Chinese pilgrims' *Travels* know.

Agencies for uniting the provinces of India.

Within the limits of India itself, province was isolated from province by differences of government, language, climate, and manners, by high hills, dense forests, and deep rivers and by the absence of roads and of easy means of conveyance. But from early Hindu times, this internal isolation was often broken and a pan- Indian community of ideas, customs and culture was created by certain agencies. These were: (i) the pilgrim-student, (ii) the soldier of fortune, (iii) the imperial conqueror, and (iv) the son-in-law imported from the centres of blue blood (such as Kanauj or Prayag for Brahmans and Mewar and Marwar in the case of Kshatriyas) for the purpose of hypergamy or raising the social status of a rich man settled among lower castes in a far-off province.

The great holy cities of the different provinces were regarded as sources of sanctity by all Indians alike. They were, besides, seats of the highest Sanskrit learning, or universities of the type of the mediæval university of Paris. Such were Benares and Nalanda, Mathura and Taxila, Ujjaini and Prayag, Kanchi and Madura, and to a lesser extent Navadwip in Bengal. The sacred streams and temples of the north were looked upon with veneration and a lifelong yearning to visit them, by the men of the south, and in the same way, Puri and Kanchi, Setubandha and Sringeri, Dwaraka and Nasik were eagerly visited by devoted pilgrims from the north of India, in spite of the immense distances to be crossed. Furthermore, for the benefit of those who could not travel, some local rivers and cities of the south were named after those of the north and regarded as equally sanctifying. Thus, Madura is the southern Mathura, and the Godavari is the southern Ganges, Ganga Godavari. Great Sanskrit scholars and saints, like Shankaracharya and Chaitanya, have passed from one end of Hindu India to another, everywhere conquering their rivals in disputation, as Samudragupta and other kings bent on *digvijaya* did in arms. This presupposed cultural uniformity.

The Hindu pilgrims and wandering Brahman students and saints formed a connecting link between the different provinces of India, and they tended to leaven the mass of their stay-at-home countrymen with some amount of community of life and thought,—though that amount was not comparable to the wholesale standardization that is going on throughout India in these days of the railway, the newspaper, the telegraph, all-India conferences for every imaginable and unimaginable purpose, and a common administrative system and cultural language.

Similarly, military adventurers, especially of the Rajput stock, penetrated into the more backward and obscure provinces in search of a career which was denied to younger brothers in their over-crowded homeland. For example, Shivaji's ancestors are said to have migrated from Chitor; Yachappa Nair (the chieftain of Satgarh, 26 miles west of Vellore), who was killed by a Mughal general in 1694, claimed descent from the Rathors of Kanauj; the State of Vizianagram was founded in the 16th century by a Rajput general of the Muslim Sultan of Golkonda.

The cultural community of all the Indian races.

The result of all these forces was that, in spite of political disunion and differences of language tradition and custom, a uniform Sanskrit stamp was printed upon the literature and thought of all the provinces of this vast country. There was unity of religion, philosophy, literary ideas and conventions, and outlook upon life, throughout Hindu India. If we take a broad and sweeping view, without being too particular, we may even go so far as to say that there has been achieved some faint approximation also in physical type and mode of life among the various races that have lived long enough in India, and fed on the same crops, drank of the same streams, basked under the same sun. Even the immigrant Indian Muslims have, in the course of centuries, received the imprint of this country and come to differ in many essential points from their brethren living in the other parts of Asia.

When we make a broad survey of India's evolution through the last four thousand years, we cannot miss the four great landmarks that stand out prominent and clear in this expanse of time. Four distinct races or creeds have, each in its own age, determined this country's destiny. The Vedic Aryans, the Buddhists, the Musalmans and the British have each introduced a new element into India, each of them has conferred gifts which have worked through the succeeding ages and modified our life and thought, no less than our political history.

The Aryans and their gifts.

We start with the Aryans, not only because they were the first in point of time among the races whose records have been preserved, but chiefly because they have succeeded in impressing the stamp of their religion, philosophy, vocabulary, literary form and tradition, administrative system, —in short, their ideas and culture, —upon the other races of India. Tribes that cannot claim with truth to have a drop of Aryan blood in their veins have' accepted the Aryan influence and tried desperately to give their ancestors an Aryan pedigree. Aryan culture, with the addition of some elements borrowed from the Dravidians, but transformed in its own way, —rules all India and gives to it an inner unity, in spite of the diversity created by our geography, ethnology and political history.

What, then, are the elements with which the Aryans have enriched Indian life? The gifts of the Aryans are six, namely,

i. A lofty spirituality which has sublimated even the non-Aryan elements borrowed in the course of that grand synthesis which is called Hinduism.
ii. The spirit of systematizing, or the methodical arrangement of every branch of thought, by a minute analysis of its parts.
iii. Ordered imagination in literary and artistic creation, as distinguished from extravagance, grotesqueness, or emotional abandon.
iv. The grading of the people into mutually exclusive castes, based upon differences of function and of supposed ancestry.

v. Honour to woman, while rejecting feminist institutions like matriarchy and polyandry, which prevailed in the south and north of the Aryan wedge driven into "the middle kingdom" or Aryavarta.

vi. The institution of hermitages, which were distinct alike from the city universities and celibate monasteries of Christian Europe.

The fusion of the Aryans and the Non-Aryans.

Let us try to visualize what followed the Aryan penetration into north-western India. It did not lead to an utter extermination of the original inhabitants of the country (as in Australia), nor to their wholesale confinement in isolated reservations (as in North America). It is now admitted by historians that the Anglo-Saxon invasion of England was not followed by a wholesale massacre or enslavement of the native Britons, but large numbers of the latter remained on their lands, though in a politically subordinate condition and a quick and complete fusion of the two races took place, the composite product being dominated by the language and institutions of the conquering minority. This has also been the case with the European colonization of Latin America. Similarly, the Vedic Aryans who conquered the Panjab formed an even smaller ratio to the non-Aryans already in possession of the soil than the Angles and Saxons did to the Britons. Most of the Aryan new comers had to take non-Aryan wives, if they were to have any wives at all.

A grand compromise with the non-Aryan religions and customs was thus forced on the conquerors by the circumstances. Some non-Aryan gods and religious rites were accepted by them, but made purer and more philosophical. The old Vedic religion, which was entirely ritualistic and the special possession of particular tribes, now gave place to that all-embracing but undefinable system of toleration or synthesis which we call Hinduism, and which shelters within its capacious bosom every form of belief and practice that will agree to its few general conventions. The absorption of alien races and creeds into Hindu society has gone on in historic times, and has failed only in the case of rigidly exclusive creeds like Islam and Christianity, as will be explained later in the course of these lectures.

Hinduism a synthesis of religions.

The cult of the snake, once universal throughout India and now surviving among the aborigines and in the Dravidian south, and the adoration of rude stones as manifestations of the deity, —either as the *Shiva-linga* or as the Shalagram, —are clearly aboriginal faiths which the Aryans adopted with necessary modifications and made parts of the new common creed of the two races. The southern non-Aryan god Shiva, —the patron of the Ceylonese king

Ravan, —was declared to be another name of the Vedic Rudra, though the functions and attributes of the latter were quite different from Shiva's. But the coarser elements of the original Shiva worship were purged away from the composite faith. The nagas took a subordinate place in the Hindu pantheon, as attendants on the gods or as good kings. The round pebble picked up from the bed of the Gandak river and adored by local tribes, now became an emblem of Vishnu the Preserver. The old popular creeds were thus spiritualized and the rude aboriginal gods were, by the invention of new legends and allegorical interpretations, invested with the halo of a loftier philosophy.

How the Aryan mind dominates Indian thought.

In the domain of thought, the Aryans created a far-reaching revolution by introducing system or methodical arrangement into everything that they handled. The sutra literature is the best example of scientific division and orderly arrangement of rules with a rigid economy of words in the various branches of human knowledge then in the possession of the Aryans. They wrote systematic treatises on medicine, philosophy, polity, grammar, metrics, law, astronomy, ritual etc. Panini's grammar gives the most scientific treatment of a language known anywhere in the world. In art, the Indo-Aryans had not the fertility of invention and exuberant imagination of the Dravidians but what imagination they displayed was restrained and refined, though they did not approach the perfect order of form and chaste elegance of beauty for which the Aryans of Greece still stand unrivalled among mankind. This point will become clear when we contrast the latest Vedic literature and the sutras with the heterogeneous medley of fact and fiction created much later under local and preponderantly non-Aryan influence and designated as the Purans, in which we find imagination running riot.

The ancient hermitages and their work.

But the most powerful and most beneficent factor of Aryan influence consisted in the hermitages of the rishis, which grew up in what is popularly called the epic age, i.e., after the Aryans had advanced to the fertile Gangetic valley and established large and rich kingdoms, with crowded cities and magnificent Courts, and peace and leisure for the population.

The hermits or *rishis* who lived in these forest homes (*tapobans*) were not lonely recluses or celibate anchorites cut off from the society of women and the duties of the family. They formed groups of householders, living with their wives and children, but not pursuing wealth or fame or material advancement like the ordinary men of the world. All their attention was devoted to the practice of virtue and the cultivation of knowledge. Thus, they lived in the world, but were not of it. They had frequent touch with the cities and the royal Court by means of respectful invitations to the domestic ceremonies of the kings and rich men, and the visits made by the latter to these hermitages in the spirit of pilgrimage, or for taking counsel with the holy men [*Raghuvamsam,* I. 35]. The quiet repose of these sylvan retreats tempted kings and queens to retire to them in the evening of their lives.* The pupils of the sages were their own children and also boys from the busy world, who lived with the hermits, shared their toils, studied under them, and served them like their own sons. Then, when their education was completed, they would bow down to their *guru*, pay their thanks offering (*dakshina*) and come back to the busy world to take their places among the men of action. [Raghu., v. 10.]

---

*Sakuntala, when sent away to be the queen of Dushmanta, is promised retirement to the peaceful hermitage of her foster-father, after she and her husband had done their life's work and installed their son on the throne. [Sakuntala, Act IV.] So, too, another queen, Sita, in the longings that fill an expectant mother's heart, asks to be taken to the hermitages on the bank of the Ganges [Raghu., XIV. 28.]'

Thus, the ancient Hindu university, without being rigidly isolated, was kept at a safe distance from the noisy luxurious capitals and gave the purest form of physical intellectual and moral culture possible at any early age, (with the exception of natural science and mechanics). Learning was developed by the rishis, who were maintained in learned leisure partly by their pupils' foraging in the ownerless woods and fields of that age and partly by the gifts of kings and rich householders.

These hermitages were as effectual for the promotion of knowledge and the growth of serious literature as the cathedrals of medieval Europe but without the unnatural monachism of the latter.

The hermitages: their services to morality.

Lecky remarks about the celibate clergy of the Catholic world: "The effect of the mortification of the domestic affections upon the general character was probably very pernicious...In Protestant countries, where the marriage of the clergy is fully recognized, it has indeed been productive of the greatest and most unequivocal benefits. Nowhere does Christianity assume a more beneficial or a more winning form than in those gentle clerical households which stud our land, constituting, as Coleridge said, 'the one idyl of modern life,' the most perfect type of domestic peace, the centre of civilization in the remotest village... Among the Catholic priesthood, on the other hand, where the vow of celibacy is faithfully observed, a character of a different type is formed, which with very grave and deadly faults combines some of the noblest excellences to which humanity can attain." {*History of European Morals,* cabinet ed., ii. 137, 334-835). These faults were avoided in ancient India.

The ancient Brahmans enjoyed popular veneration and social supremacy, but they used their influence and prestige solely for the promotion of learning and religion, and not for enriching themselves or gratifying their passions. The nation as a whole benefited by this arrangement. But it was possible only in a purely Hindu State, without a dense population and with science and technical arts in a simple undeveloped condition.

In the calm of these sylvan retreats were developed our systems of philosophy, ethics, theology and even several branches of literature proper. Witness the vivid scenes of discussion on political science and morality in the Naimish forest, as described in the *Mahabharat, Shanti-parva.*

Herein lay the true spring-head of the ancient civilization of the Hindus, and this we owe entirely to the Indo-Aryans of the earliest or Brahmanic age.

II

THE WORK OF BUDDHISM IN INDIA

How Buddhism arose.

The initial force of Aryan civilization was spent by the time that it reached the western frontier of Bengal; Or, it would be more correct to say, that the new elements that had entered into Aryan society caused a great transformation of its original character. In Mithila or North Bihar, the Brahman ascendancy in thought was lost and the Kshatriyas began to think and act for themselves and to resist the Brahmanic supremacy. Some scholars* have called it the Kshatriya revolt against the Brahmans, but it should rather be styled an inevitable new stage in the evolution of India.

A high philosophy, quite distinct from the Vedic religion, was developed first in the hermitages and then at the Courts of Kshatriya kings like Janaka, and it led, in the course of time, to the rise of a great Kshatriya preacher. It was Gautam Buddha, the lion of the Sakya clan, who rose in open protest against the power and ritual of the Brahmans and thus introduced a new force into Indian life and thought.

* Muir's Sanskrit Texts, Vol. I (3rd. ed.) 296-479. The contest originated much earlier before the caste system bad become rigid.

The gifts of Buddhism.

Let us consider the gifts of Buddhism to India. They were six in number: —

i. Buddhism gave us a popular religion without any complicated and unintelligible ritual such as could be performed only by a priestly class. It deliberately set itself to appeal to the masses, and wonderfully succeeded in winning their hearts by its simplicity, its emotional element, its easy ethical code, its use of the vernacular language in its scriptures, its popular method of teaching by means of parables, its worship in congregation. It introduced a personal element into religion, in the form of a known human Saviour, in the place of the impersonal forces of

Nature to whom the Vedic Aryans used to pray and the passionless abstract deity adored in the Upanishads.

ii. Image-worship was most probably introduced into India by the Buddhists. We can easily conjecture that the earliest statues of Buddha were set up as purely commemorative of a great master and preacher, but that they soon came to be worshipped as representations of the godhead. For sheltering these sacred images houses had to be built, and thus temples arose, while the Vedic Aryans had been content with offering sacrifices on altars in the open air, as was the case with the Aryans of ancient Persia.

iii. The monastic system or the organization of religious devotees in disciplined communities or orders was another innovation due to Buddhism. It is true that solitary recluses and old men retiring to forests in order to end their days in lonely contemplation, had been known in India before the rise of Buddhism, but not the banding together of religious devotees into a fraternity of monks, obeying a common head and living together under a common code of disciplinary rules.

iv. Buddhism created a vast and varied literature in the spoken tongue, which was meant for the common people and not reserved like a sacred language for a learned priesthood.

v. The most charming contributions of Buddhism to Indian life were in the domain of sculpture and architecture. Here was a new element which the Vedic Aryans had not thought of and which, though introduced by the Buddhists, continued with growing volume in the later Hindu period. The Buddhists set the example of dedicating cave temples, which the Hindus and Jainas followed in after ages.

vi. Buddhism established an intimate contact between India and foreign countries. This religion was India's greatest gift to the outer world. It was a universal movement, a force irrespective of country and caste, which the whole ancient East was free to accept. Indian monks and scholars carried Buddhism to foreign countries from the third century before Christ onwards and thereafter the converts of these countries looked up to India as a holy land, the cradle of their faith, a pilgrimage to which was the crowning act of a pious householder's life.*

*Rockhill's Life of Buddha from the Tibetan; S. C. Das's Indian Pandits in the Land of Snow; Aymonier's L'e Cambodge; P. Bagchi's Le Canon Bouddhique en Chine.

India's isolation how broken in the Buddhist age.

Thus, there were two streams of human movement, one composed of our native Buddhist teachers going out of India and another of foreign Buddhist pilgrims and students flocking to India, which broke our isolation in that age. The

Hindus followed the example thus set, and from the third century after Christ we have records of Hindu missionaries and colonists settling in Further India and several of the Pacific islands.

The result was that, in what is called the Buddhistic age the fusion of foreign non-Aryan immigrant tribes and families with the Indian population became an easy occurrence of every day. History records many examples of it. In the first century of the Christian era, some families that bear Persian names are found settled in Western India and patronizing Brahmans and Buddhist monks alike. The Karle and Nasik cave inscriptions tell us that Harapharna (i.e., Holophernes), son of Setapharna, a Sova-Saka, gave away a cave-hall surrounded by nine cells to the Mahasanghika branch of Buddhist monks and that Ushavadata (i.e., Rishava-datta) a Saka, the son-in-law of the Kshatrapa Nahapana (another Persian name), gave away three lakhs of cows and sixteen villages to the Brahmans, paid for the marriage of eight Brahman maidens, fed a lakh of Brahmans for one year, dedicated a cave-monastery for the use of the Buddhist begging friars, and made a gift of the villages of Karanjika for the support of the ascetics living in the caves at Valuraka, without distinction of sect (Epigr. Indica, VII. 58, 72; viii. 78, 86). In later times, when Buddhism decayed, these foreign settlers were quietly and completely absorbed in the mass of the Hindu population, their foreign origin having been forgotten during their long previous stay in India.

Thus Buddhism, without at first intending it, contributed very largely to the synthesis which has produced the modern Hindu society.

In this expansion of India outside and consolidation within, Asoka had made the first beginnings in the third century before Christ; but the movement became vast and sweeping only in the first century after Christ, under the Scythians and the Bactrian Greeks and Indo-Parthians whom the Scythians absorbed and replaced in political domination.

How foreign races were Indianized and Hinduized.

Mahayan Buddhism advanced conquering the minds of men to the west, north-west and north out of India, while the Kushan emperors penetrated with their arms from Central Asia south-eastwards into the Gangetic valley. Thus, these two forces, physical and spiritual, had the same effect of bringing foreign settlers into India, putting the Indian stamp on them, and finally converting their descendants into unmistakable Hindus a few centuries afterwards. The Sulaiman range ceased to exist as a barrier on our west and the Panjab and Afghanistan, Khurasan and Seistan became as one country.

The ports of our west coast, —Sopara, Cambay, Broach and Chaul, — facilitated the same immigration by sea and Konkan and Gujrat and even Malwa became the homes of foreign tribes that accepted the culture and religion of the land of their adoption. Witness the satraps of Ujjaini. Chashtana, the founder of this line, was the son of Psamotika, a name which we find in the dynastic lists of ancient Egypt and Babylonia alike. But his descendants soon became Hindus and patrons of the Hindu religion.

The new comers into India retained their un-Hindu foreign names and customs for some time, because Buddhism did not insist on uniformity in these points, but embraced all within its tolerant' bosom. After a few generations, however, when the Hindu revival began, the descendants of these foreigners were hammered or coaxed into uniformity with the Hindus around them in name, in social practices and in manners and a homogeneous population and culture in India was the result. Thus, the Andhra king Sri Pulumayi, the son of Vashishti, is praised for having brought society back to the rigid purity of Hindu law by "stopping *mesalliances* between the four castes" through the extermination of the casteless Kshaharata dynasty of satraps,

Khakkarata—vasa—niravasesa—karasa

vinivatita—chaturvama—sakamsa—

(Epigr. Indica, viii. 60). And yet this king gave a village to the Sramanas or Buddhist priests of the Bhatayaniya fraternity, living in the Queen's cave *(Ibid., p. 67).*

So, too, the earlier rulers of the Kushan empire in India bear purely Turki names, like Kujula Kadphisa, Vajeski, Kaniski and Huviski but immediately after Huviski we have the clear Hindu name of Vasudeva.

The Mongolian Ahom dynasty that conquered Assam in the thirteenth century, at first used non-Indian names like Sudangpha (1397), Supimpha (1493), Suhangmung (1497), Sukhampha (1552) and then from the beginning of the 17th century their descendants became Hindu Rajahs with names like Pratap Sinha (1603), Jayadhwaja (1648), Udayaditya (1669), Rudra Sinha (1696), etc.

At first the Scythians (Sakas) in India used to keep up their connection with their far-off homeland west of the Bolan Pass. Thus, the Mathura lion-capital of the first century A.D. bears an inscription in honour of all the inhabitants of the Saka-land: *Sarvasa sakarastanasa puyae (Epigr. Indica, ix. 146).*

Now, this Sanskrit word *Saka-sthan*, became *Sekestene* in Greek, *Sejistan* in mediaeval Persian and *Seistan* in modern Persian. It is a province in the south-eastern corner of Persia.

But a few generations later we find the Sakas completely naturalized in India and absorbed into the Hindu population. So, too, the Hun invaders of the fifth century A.D., after many fights with the Gupta empire, lost the chance of political domination in India and settled down as peaceful common people, contributing tribes to various Hindu castes and professions. Thus, one recognized Rajput clan bears the name of Hun. Their nomadic brethren, the Gujars, after many wanderings since their migration to India, have settled in the Delhi district and the country West of it and given their name to the province of Gujrat or Gurjara-rashtra, the district of Gujranwala, and to the Rajput clan of Bar-Gujars.

How later Hindu society became rigid.

After the upheaval caused by the mass incursions of the Scythians and other nomadic races, from the first to the sixth century of the Christian era, Hindu society was reorganized and graded anew. The caste grouping then adopted became stereotyped in every province. History has preserved no record of how this happened, nor the names of the mighty social leaders and Brahman scholars who imposed their will on such a huge population throughout such an immense extent of country and poured the fluid elements of Hindu society into a mould where they have acquired rigidity for all time to come. But we get a few glimpses from the identical tradition preserved in places as far apart as Gujrat, Assam, Lower Bengal and Orissa.* In each of these provinces there is a universally accepted belief that an ancient king wanted to perform a Vedic sacrifice but found the local Brahmans ignorant of the scriptures and unclean in their lives (like the English clergy of the earlier years of king Alfred), so that he had to induce five pure Brahmans from Kanauj to come and settle in his kingdom, and from these five immigrants the best local Brahman families of later times trace their descent.

* *Imp, Gazetteer of India* 3rd ed. ii. 307; Bengali tradition about king Adisur; *Bombay Gazetteer*, Ist ed., ix. pt. it, P- 7.

At that forgotten reorganization of Hindu society, the passion everywhere was to revert to the pristine purity of blood, — at least to the standard of social practice and religious rites, —that had existed before the Hun flood submerged North India, and the seat of this pure type was Kanauj in Madhyadesh or the Ganga-Jamuna doab.

This huge reconstruction of Hindu society stretches, with its ebb and flow, from the sixth to the tenth century after Christ. During this period the Scythian and other foreign settlers were completely Hinduized, the Rajputs rose to kingship as the ruling caste, with their numberless principalities covering the whole country from Attock and Und on the Indus to Palamau in South Bihar. They made themselves the ardent champions of the new Hinduism. It was on this Rajput wall that the Muslim invaders from the northwest impinged at the close of the tenth century.

The elevating power of Hinduism.

This moral transformation of savage foreigners is the greatest glory of India and a proof of the death-defying vitality of Hinduism, considered not as a dogmatic creed (which it never was) but as a social force and civilizing agency. The spirit of India has triumphed over time and change and kept the composite Indian people's mind as active and keen as in the best days of pure Aryan ascendancy. The blending of races here has not led to that intellectual and moral deterioration which is found among the present-day mixed population of what was once Spanish America.

As a distinguished orientalist has truly observed, "The most important fact in Hindu history is overlooked (by our orthodox writers). I mean the attractive power of Hindu civilization, which has enabled it to assimilate and absorb into itself every foreign invader except the Moslem and the European. Those Indians have a poor idea of their country's greatness, who do not realize how it has tamed and civilized the nomads of Central Asia, so that wild Turkoman tribes have been transformed into some of the most famous of the Rajput royal races." [A. M. T. Jackson in Indian Antiquary, 1910, p. 77].

III

THE LIFE STORY OF BUDDHISM IN INDIA

The history of Buddhism in India is a story of strange transformations running through twenty centuries. The astonishing result of it is that this religion, which has converted nearly a quarter of the human race, has totally disappeared from the land of its birth. But all the stages of this growth, transformation, decay and death can be historically traced.

Original Buddhism only a new form of Hinduism.

In its origin, Buddhism was not avowedly a new creed but an appeal for holier living in the bosom of the existing Hindu religion and society. Buddha was not a prophet but a saint, who urged his hearers to give up their vices and follies and to practise that purity of conduct and sincerity of belief which is the essence of every true religion. He himself, so far as we can judge from the scanty volume of what may be considered as his true sayings, taught neither new dogmas, nor new rituals, nor a new philosophy. *

The basic doctrine of Buddhism, as all scholars now admit, sprang from the pre-existing Hindu philosophy of the Sankhya and the later Upanishads, —the belief, namely, that human life is a misery which is multiplied by the same soul passing through a cycle of rebirths, and the cessation of rebirth is the means of extinguishing that misery. Such cessation comes from moral self-control and the repression of all desires. The eightfold path enjoined by Buddha for this purpose is only a code of general ethics and not the special creed of a revealed and distinctive faith.

As Kern points out, "It does not necessarily follow that the Buddha was supposed to have invented the whole of morality. On the contrary, the Master himself repeatedly extols the morals and virtues of the ancient rishis... Buddhism has wisely adopted many articles of morality and pious customs flowing from the sources of the Brahmanist code.....The sect originally had no moral code at all, except the prohibitions and duties prescribed to the members of the Order.'" [*Manual of Indian Buddhism,* 68-69].

* Kern's *Manual*, p. 47— "We only surmise that both systems (*viz*,, the Buddhist and the Sankhya) derive from a common remote source." Also p.* 50 middle.

Thus, so far as the original philosophy of Buddhism goes, there is hardly any break of continuity between Buddha and the Hindu sages who had preceded him. In the *Jatakas* Buddha says again and again that true piety consists not in the performance of rites or the repetition of set prayers but in holy living and holy dying.

Then, again, in the proclamations of the great royal preacher Asoka, we see the same insistence on general morality as the real aim of the Buddhistic *Dhamma*. In the second Pillar Edict Asoka says, "Dharma is good but what is Dharma? It consists in doing good to the many, kindness, charity, truthfulness, purity."*

Dharmah sadhuh—kim astu dharma iti apasrabam bahukalyanam, daya, danam satyam, shucham.

The definition of *Dharma* is even more explicit in the ninth Rock Edict: —

"Dharma has great fruits. It consists in much kindness to slaves and servants, reverence to elders, control of the passions, almsgiving to Sramanas and Brahmanas and to others similar benefit of Dharma."

So much for the new creed on its doctrinal side.

Nor did Buddha lay down a special ritual for his followers. That was of later growth. The only new thing he introduced was the institution of the orders of monks and nuns. But even the rules of monastic discipline seem to have been left by him few, simple and undefined. They had to be codified and stiffened after his death. This is clearly proved by the traditions relating to the first Council held immediately after his death and still more by the story of the second Council, that of Vaisali, the calling together of which would not have been necessary if the rules of monastic life had been fully elaborated and laid down in writing, so as to obviate all doubt and controversy about their nature. [Kern, 103; Rockhill's *Life of Buddha,* 171-180.]

With the disappearance of the towering personality of its founder, began the long line of changes in Buddhism. First, an attempt, —a very natural attempt was made to set up a scripture and a code of recorded rules in the place of the living teacher who had disappeared and his sayings which had till then been orally preserved. Immediately after the death of Buddha, five hundred monks assembled at Rajgir, under the presidency of the aged Maha-Kasyapa, for this purpose.

"Kasyapa the Great, whom the Master had designated as his successor, made the proposal that the brethren should assemble to rehearse the Lord's precepts. The proposal was adopted." [Kern, 102, 103; Rockhill, 157-160; Beal, ii. 162.]

Split in the Buddhist Community.

But it was a hopeless attempt to reach uniformity by means of a council of bishops, without an ever-present infallible Pope or dictator of the faith. A hundred years after the first Council, difference of opinion as to the orthodox doctrines and practices, made the summoning of a second Council necessary. The scandalous lives and heretical doctrines of the monks of Vaisali, roused the indignation of the reformer Yasas, and he was supported by the venerable priests Sarvaka and Revata. But it was to no effect. The Vaisali Council, instead of restoring uniformity to the Church, broke up in disorder; two different Councils seem to have been held here by the two parties, neither recognizing the authority of the other, and the Church was rent by an open schism. [Kern, 103-109; Rockhill, 171-172; Watters, ii. 73-77.]

From the legends of the Vaisali Council we see how the moral canker had begun to eat into the vitals of Buddhism. The founder of the faith had preached it over a small tract of land from the Nepal Terai to Gaya and from Allahabad to Patna. It had been honoured by kings and merchants but along with Hinduism and not to the exclusion of the latter faith. It had, therefore, gained no preponderance, even in this narrow tract of land, either in the number of its followers or in the wealth of its Church.

Wealth and Moral Degeneration of the Buddhist Monks.

But, in time the monasteries began to grow rapidly in accumulated wealth from gifts. Only three hundred years after Buddha's death, we find startling examples of the costly donations to his Church in the stories of Asoka's dotage.

The Chinese pilgrim Yuan Chwang narrates the story thus:

"King Asoka having fallen sick, desired to offer all his possessions [to the Buddhist monks], so as to crown his religious merit. The minister who was carrying on the government was unwilling to comply with his wish. Sometime after this, as he was eating part of an amalaka fruit, he playfully put the half of it for an offering.

Then the king commanded an attendant officer to come and addressed him thus: 'Take this half fruit and offer it to the priest in the Kukkutaram monastery and speak thus to the venerable ones — All that I have is gone and lost, only this half fruit remains as my little possession.' " [Beal, ii. 95; Watters, ii. 99.] Here the king built a great stupa, named the Amalaka. The story is also repeated by Ashwa-ghosha.

Wealth gave leisure to the Church and the monkish brain devoted its well-endowed leisure to the weaving of minute subtleties of doctrine and the elaboration of ritual, under which the founder's simple faith and code of practical ethics were completely buried. A very complex philosophy and cosmogony of their own was evolved by the Buddhist theologians in their monastic repose. They created a new and vast religious literature like the Vaishnav Goswami's of Bengal in the 16th and 17th centuries. But as no two philosophers are ever found to agree, these metaphysical subtleties led to quarrels, and the Church broke up into a multitude of sub-sects, each under a leader and each proclaiming war against the other followers of the same faith. We learn that soon after Buddha's nirvan and even before Asoka made Buddhism a world-religion, its followers had become divided into four main sects. Their internal dissensions went on increasing with the spread of the faith. Before the first century of the Christian era, the number of recognized sub-divisions had increased io eighteen, besides probably many hundred smaller personal groups. As Yuan Chwang, in the 7th century, mournfully noted, "The different [Buddhistic] schools are constantly at variance, and their contending utterances rise like angry waves of the sea. The different sects have their separate masters. There are eighteen schools, each claiming pre-eminence." [Beal, i. 80.] For some time before this Chinese pilgrim's visit, the various schools had been grouped under two main divisions, the Mahayan and Hinayan but it did not improve matters. These two sects hated each other more bitterly than either of them hated the Hindus.

In Ceylon, the jealousy and antipathy between the great rival monasteries, the Mahavihar and Abhayagiri, led to constant dissension and occasional persecution, such as the destruction of the Mahavihar in the reign of King Mahasena (c. 300 A.D.)

Thus, the unity of the Buddhist Church was broken and at the same time moral decay resulted from the increased wealth, indolence, and luxury of the monks. The lavish benefactions of Asoka and Kanishka and the position of supreme respect in the State given by these emperors to the Buddhist monks, were, in reality, a curse rather than a blessing to the faith. In the Saranath edict Asoka threatens expulsion from the order and unfrocking to those monks, who would introduce schism into the Church.

During what we call the Buddhist period, Hinduism was neither dead nor silent. It may have lost the royal patronage under certain kings; it may have produced no great scholar or saint for a generation or two. But only half a century after Asoka's death, when his dynasty was overthrown, Hinduism raised its head and soon recovered its ascendancy. This was effected not by its persecuting or penalizing the Buddhists but by producing greater scholars, better authors, nobler saints, and finer artists, and above all by practising greater active piety or philanthropy, —in respect of which Buddhism had lost the superiority it had held in its founder's lifetime or in Asoka's reign.

Intellectual decline of the Buddhists in India.

The intellectual decline of the Buddhist priests in Asoka's own capital is well illustrated by a story narrated by Yuan Chwang in connection with the Stupa of sounding the ghanta. He writes:

"At first there were about a hundred Sangharamas in this city; the priests were grave and learned, and of high moral character. The scholars among the heretics (i.e. Hindus) were silent and dumb. But afterwards when that generation of priests had died out, their successors were not equal to those gone before. Then the teachers of the heretics, during the interval, gave themselves up to earnest study with a view to mastery. Whereupon they summoned their partisans to assemble together within the priests' precincts, and then they addressed them, saying with a loud voice, 'Strike loudly the ghanta and summon all the learned men [i.e., Buddhist monks] If we are wrong, let them overthrow us.'

They then addressed the king and asked him to decide between the weak and the strong . . . And now the heretical masters were men of high talent and marked learning; the [Buddhist] priests, although numerous, were weak in their verbal discussion. The heretics said, 'We have got the victory. From this time forth let no Sangharama dare to sound the ghanta to call together a congregation.' The king confirmed this result of the discussion. . . For twelve years the ghanta was not sounded."* [Beal, ii. 96-97. Watters, ii. 100.]

*And then came a Buddhist champion, but only from Southern India!

The wise leaders of the Hindu revival, while they beat the Buddhists by avoiding barren philosophical subtleties and the jarring of sect with sect, and by showing greater love and care for the suffering lower classes, —also cut the ground from under the feet of Buddhism, by stealing several of its practices which appeal to the human heart and imagination. Thus, image-worship and the car-procession were most probably borrowed by the Hindus from Buddhism. In the fourth century, Fa Hien noticed a car-procession exactly like our own in the Buddhist monasteries of Khotan. [Beal, i. xxvi.]

By the beginning of the seventh century A.D., this policy of new Hinduism had already so far crippled Buddhism that Yuan Chwang noticed Hindu temples outnumbering Buddhist monasteries in an increasing proportion, as he proceeded from the Panjab to Bengal, i.e., through the very province of Buddha's missionary labours.

What did the leaders of Indian-Buddhism do in the face of this growing-strength of their foes? They did not abate their internal quarrels one jot. They produced no outstanding scholar or saint for work in India. Even the royal patronage enjoyed by Buddhism during Harsha's reign was, but the last flicker of a dying lamp as regards the hopes of Buddhism.

The Pala kings of Bengal who rose to power a century after Harsha and held sway for three hundred years were no doubt Buddhists but they equally patronized Hindu scholars and holy men. Their ministers and courtiers included Hindus no less than Buddhists, and the Sanskrit books and exquisite statuary produced under them were on Hindu subjects as much as on Buddhistic. Hindus and Buddhists alike studied the grammar of Panini and cultivated Sanskrit logic in this period, as the medieval Sanskrit literature recovered from Nepal and Tibet richly shows.

The Buddhists reaped the benefit of their great universities at Nalanda and Vikramshila. We know of no Hindu university in the North, but many rich Hindu householders and kings maintained Sanskrit pandits who fed and taught their personal groups of pupils in their homes, as was the practice in India down to our own days.

Mahaya Buddhism, its aim and work.

The Mahayan school had during the first seven centuries of the Christian era produced a vast mass of literature, both religious and secular, but in Sanskrit. It is very little known in India, because the best workers in this field have been Frenchmen and Germans.* An immense and varied mass of materials on the subject has been added by the recent discoveries of Stein, Le Coq, Pelliot and others in Turkestan, Khotan and Mongolia.

* A useful summary in translation is available in Mr. G. K. Nariman's *Literary History of Sanskrit Buddhism*. Also R. L. *Mitra's Nepalese Bud. Lit.*

The Mahayan school is of very great interest as forming a bridge, or rather a half-way house, between the old Buddhism and modern Hinduism. The doctrine of the Mahayan was intensely human and practical. Its monks did not all bury themselves in the seclusion of their cells, each seeking to attain his personal salvation by becoming a passionless arhat. They revived the active philanthropy which Buddha had preached in every Jataka parable. It was essentially a religion of the service of man, though at the same time it produced great scholars, too. It was a very popular religion, because it made an irresistible appeal to the emotions by its gorgeous ritual, its preaching the cult of bhakti or devotion to a personal saviour (Bodhisattva), its programme of active humanitarianism, as distinct from lonely contemplation and self-mortification.

What was the essence of Mahayan Buddhism? In the curious evolution and transformation of his religion in the course of many centuries, Buddha the living preacher had long ago ceased to be regarded as a human being. He had become a god, or rather the king of the gods, too high above us to be approached by mortals directly. He was now a dread shadow or supreme name only, hidden within the halo of his power and sanctity and not a deity to be gazed at or addressed by mankind. Therefore, we sinners must send our petitions to him through his courtiers and constant servitors. These were Bodhisattvas or men who by the practice of piety, self-control and sacrifice for the good of others, in successive births through millions of years, had been gradually rising higher and higher in the scale of being, and who would after millions of years more reach the finality of their development as perfect Buddhas. In short, they were Buddhas in the making and therefore could best act as intercessors between sinning men and the great Buddha. Hence, in Mahayan, the worship of Bodhisattvas practically superseded that of 'Buddha himself, and the votive statues of the former almost drove those of the latter out of the field, as archaeological excavations in the chief Mahayan sites show.

Mahayan was an intensely living and active faith. It came forth into the world, visiting the homes of the people instead of seeking cloistered seclusion, sanctimonious aloofness from others, and intellectual pride, as was generally the case with Hinayan. Therefore, Hinayan was, in comparison with it, unprogressive, coldly intellectual, inert, and rather monotonous through lack of variety and influence over human conduct.

By this I do not mean to assert that Mahayan had no ascetics and theological writers of its own. I mean to say that the meditative side of Mahayan was not everything; the millions of laymen were reached by its practical side or philanthropy.

New Hinduism absorbs the best elements of Buddhism.

When the new Hinduism asserted itself after the reorganization of the social grades in the 7th and 8th centuries after Christ, the monastic and contemplative elements of Mahayan Buddhism were borrowed by the Shaivas and the devotional and humanitarian elements by the Vaishnavs. In consequence, Buddhism disappeared from India by being swallowed up and completely absorbed by the new Hinduism. There is hardly any difference traceable between Shiva the Yogi of Hindu mythology and the Dhyani Buddha of later Mahayan. The car procession of the three idols,* the gorgeous worship in temples, the cult of bhakti or personal love for God as man, the active service of the poor (in whom the God Narayan is believed to incarnate Himself) and the preaching friars of the new and revived Vaishnavism of the 8th century, —these were the weapons taken from the Buddhists which conquered the decaying Buddhism because of the superior energy and fervour of neo-Hinduism.

*Jagannath, Balaram, and Subhadra. Compare Fa Hien's description, "They made a four-wheeled image-car, more than thirty cubits high...The chief image stood in the middle of the car, with two Bodhisattvas in attendance oil it' (Legge's tr., p. 19). A mediaeval Oriya poem on the idol Jagannath, named Daru-brahma, states "The god carved out of wood, Jagannath, reigns on the throne in the form of Buddha, without hands feet or toes...I am Buddha incarnate, I shall protect the people of the Kali era' (Canto V.)

The decaying or abandoned monasteries of the Buddhists were taken possession of by the Shaiva monks and raised their heads again as Hindu maths, e.g., the Bodh Gaya temple itself, which Yuan Chwang had found overgrown with jungles and almost deserted in 634 was appropriated by Shaiva monks of the Giri section. The Vaishnav Bairagis replaced the philanthropic Mahayan sramanas. The neighbouring people hardly felt the change, it was so slight; the thing was the same, only the name of the god was different and a new set of men, clad in the same long yellow robes were performing the same worship!

And even the name of the god was not really changed in the transformed Hinduism of the time, because Buddha was finally given a place in, the Hindu pantheon as the eighth incarnation of Vishnu. As the Vaishnav poet Jayadev (12th century) sings:

"Thou dost condemn the sacrifices enjoined by the Vedas, as thy heart is filled with pity at the sight of the slaughter of animals. O Vishnu, incarnate in the form of Buddha!"'*

The Shivalinga at Saranath, a short distance from the Asoka stupa, is even now known as Shiva Sangheshwar, i.e., the Lord of the Sangha or the third member of the Buddhist Trinity.' †

* Nindasi yajna-bidher ahaha shrutijatam

Sadaya-hridaya darshita pashu-ghatam

Keshva dhrita-Buddha-sharira! [Gita-govinda]

†Jaynarayan Ghoshal's Kashi Parikrama (written about 1792) speaks of Hindus worshipping the Sangheshwar linga after crossing the Varuna River. This name also occurs in the Kashi Mahatmya.

Tantrikism, how it arose and what it did.

In the last stage of Mahayan the transition from Buddhism to Hinduism was rendered imperceptible by the agency of Tantrikism.

In going out of North India to convert millions of primitive Mongolians in Tibet, Central Asia, and China, neither the pure ethics of Buddhism as taught by the founder, nor the subtle philosophy woven by the rich and leisured monks in the Gangetic valley was found to be of practical use. Success could be attained in mass conversions of such magnitude only by stooping down to the intellect and familiar practices of the converts. [Compare the policy of Roberto de Nobili in Southern India.] The Buddhist preachers in these new lands made a compromise and adopted the animism or spirit-worship which was the prevailing religion of the Mongolians and merely superimposed the Buddhist pantheon on it, i.e., they gilded spirit-worship with a thin coating of Buddhistic doctrines and gave Buddhistic names to the locally adored spirits. This Tantrik worship gradually developed an iconography, a philosophy, and a literature of its own in Tibet and East Bengal.

The aim of Tantra was to acquire control over the spirits by the practice of austerities and elaborate mystic rites, and then to use this supernatural power for the gratification of the senses, the transmutation of the baser metals into gold, and the production of potent medicines by magic, as well as salvation for the soul.

The gods and goddesses of Tantrik Buddhism became the deities of the Shaiva form of Hinduism. Thus, the Buddhist Tara was identified as the Shakti or female energy of Shiva and adored as a Hindu goddess. The dreaded Kali and other *maha-vidyas* are further examples of this borrowing of cults.

Tantrikism was the most widely prevalent and popular religion of North and East Bengal* from the 8th to the 12th century and even later. Whether this Tantrik population should be called Buddhist or Hindu was a quarrel over words only. The people did not feel any change when they described themselves as Hindus instead of Buddhists, in an imaginary census return of the time.

* A Bengali priest of Shiva was given extensive lands in the Guntur district (Madras) in 1261 A.D., by Queen Rudramba of the Kakatiya dynasty. Another Shaiva priest from Bengal was the guru of King Amrita-pal of the Rashtrakuta dynasty and appointed head of a monastery in the Gangetic doab, c. 1220, as the Badayun inscription records.

In Central and Western Bengal Tantrikism was practised but not as the predominant religion. Buddhism in other forms lingered there as late as the sixteenth century. The researches of Dr. Haraprasad Shastri have recovered this lost page of our religious history and established the fact on unassailable evidence.

How later Hinduism converted the Buddhist masses in India.

With the moral decline of their monks and the failure of the Church in India to produce great scholars and saints, the latter-day Buddhist congregation in India were left as sheep without a shepherd. Their actual religion lost its highly intellectual or esoteric character and continued as a mere faith of the populace with traditions and practices that were blindly followed, and this latest Buddhism in Bengal and Bihar took its place by the side of the worship of the village godlings under ignorant quacks as priests. The Buddhistic ritual probably continued to be followed but in ignorance of the philosophy underlying it. Thus, Buddhism in its last stage in India ceased to be a fiving and growing faith because it could no longer produce an expanding and perpetually modernized literature and a fresh stream of teachers in every generation.

The upper classes of society, especially in the towns, went over to Hinduism very early and the faith of Buddha lingered in the villages and out-of-the-way places. (Compare the state of paganism in the Roman empire after Constantine the Great).

The work of the great preachers of neo-Hinduism illustrated.

The conversion of the later Indian Buddhists to Hinduism was effected by some giant intellects among the neo-Hindu scholars. Shankaracharya, (circa 800 A. D.), by his invincible logical power and scriptural knowledge defeated all the Buddhist theologians that he met from Cape Comorin to the Ganges. Ramanuja (c. 1100) did the same in a more limited sphere. Four centuries later (1511 A. D.), Chaitanya in his pilgrimage through Southern India extinguished the last remnants of Buddhism there. As his biographer writes: — "At Vriddhachalam a very learned Buddhist professor held forth on the nine doctrines of his Church before the Master..... who argued with him in order to lower his pride. The very Buddhist philosophy of nine tenets, though rich in logical reasoning was torn to pieces by the Master's argumentation.... The great philosophers were all vanquished; the audience tittered; the Buddhists felt shame and alarm.... Their professor rose up and began to chant Hari! Hari! He did reverence to the Master, saluting him as Krishna." [J. Sarkar's tr. of Chaitanya-charitamrita, p. 76.]

Unlike Shankara and Ramanuja, Chaitanya was intensely emotional and while on the one hand he defeated the Buddhist champions of his day in learned disputations, he, on the other hand, swept the masses into his fold by the striking appeal of his lovable personality, his saintly character, and his own example of Bhakti. The priests of the older faith had been already dethroned from the hearts of their congregation, which lay vacant and ready to receive a new true Master.

Last vestiges of Buddhism in Bengal.

In Bengal, Buddhism continued in the form of Dharma worship. That this village god Dharma is only the second member of the Buddhist Trinity will become evident from the character of the rites and the attributes of the god Dharma as given in the surviving literature of this cult, namely, The Dharma Mangal, the *Shunya-Puran*, &c. The Dharma of this worship is not a Brahmanic God, his image is an earthen mound set up at the end of the village and his priests belong to the lower castes. [H. P. Shastri's Discovery of Living Buddhism in Bengal, 1898; J. A. S. B., 1894, p. 135.] A significant light is thrown upon the subject by the tradition recorded in a mediaeval Bengali poem named Niranjaner Rushna to the effect that Dharma in Heaven, feeling the oppression of the Brahmans, incarnated himself in the form of a Yavana, wearing a black cap and loose drawers, riding a powerful horse, armed with the dagger and the bow, accompanied by the lesser gods (all accoutred as Muslim warriors) and shouting the name of 'Khuda' as the sole God, sacked the city of Jaipur and demolished its Hindu-temples.* There can, therefore, be no doubt of the Dharma-puja being a survival of Buddhism.

* Niranjaner Rushna forms an additional canto in one MS. of Ramai Pandit's Shunya-Puran (a treatise on the ritual of the worship of Dharma composed in the 11th century.) This canto is a later addition (? 16th cent.)

Dr. H. P. Shastri has also adduced reasons for holding that the Sahajiya and Nyada sects of Bengal, who are commonly classed as Vaishnavs, originated from the decadent Buddhists of later times.*

* H. P. Shastri's Discovery &c.; Dharma Puja Bidhi, Bauddha Gan O Doha; J. A, S. B.,1895, pp. 55 and 65. "

The death-blow to Buddhism in the famous cities of North India and along the main highway of the Gangetic valley was given by the Muslim conquest of the 13th century. The monastery of Bihar in the Patna district was sacked, and its monks slaughtered by these invaders under the mistake that they were soldiers, as will be seen from the following Persian narrative of a contemporary writer:

"Muhammad-i-Bakhtiar organized an attack upon the fortified city of Bihar. They captured the fortress and acquired great booty. The greater number of the inhabitants of the place were Brahmans and the whole of those Brahmans had their heads shaven [these were really sramanas] and they were all slain. There were a great number of books there...On becoming acquainted [with the contents of those books], it was found that the whole of the fortress and city was a college and in the Hindui tongue they call a college a vihara." [Tabaqat-i-nasiri,tr. by Raverty, p. 520.]

Before the ceaseless eastward tide of Muslim raiders, the surviving monks of North India fled to Nepal with their books and there their sacred literature was preserved, to be collected in the 19th century by Brian H. Hodgson (the British Resident at Khatmandu, 1820-44) and sent to Paris, where it formed the source of new and most fruitful Buddhistic studies under Burnouf and his pupils.

But in obscure and out-of-the-way places in Bengal, some families continued to follow Buddhism as late as 1436 A. D., in which year a manuscript of the Bodhi-charyavatar was copied in the Bengali alphabet, in a village of the Bardwan district, by a scribe named Amitava, who is described in the colophon as a pious Buddhist (sad-bauddha-karana-kayastha-thakkura). But by the end of the 16th century, the new energy breathed into Bengali Vaishnavism by Chaitanya and his apostles and into Assamese Vaishnavism by Shankaradev and his school swept over the whole country and completed the absorption of the last remnants of the Buddhists in the land of Buddha's birth into the fold of Hinduism.

IV

THE MUSLIM SETTEELSIENT AND THE CHANGES THAT IT WROUGHT

Muslims cannot merge in Hindu Society and creed.

The Muslim conquest of India differed fundamentally from all preceding invasions in one respect. The Muslims came to India as a new element which the older inhabitants could not absorb. The Greek, Scythian, Mongolian and Parthian invaders had, a few generations after their settlement in this land, been completely Hinduized in name, speech, manners, religion, dress, and ideas.

In the second century before Christ, a Greek named Heliodoros the son of Dion, when travelling in India on an embassy, could adore Vishnu and erect a column in honour of that Hindu god. Men considered it quite natural that he should do so and take to himself the title of a Bhagavat or Vaishnav.*

*The Besnagar pillar-inscription in the Brahmi script records: — "This column, surmounted by the figure of Garuda (The bird sacred to Vishnu) was erected by Heliodoros, a Bhagavat and an inhabitant of Taxila, the son of Dion and a Greek ambassador sent by the Great King Antalkidas to 'King Bhaga-bhadra."

But Islam, is a fiercely monotheistic religion. It cannot allow any compromise with polytheism or admit a plurality of deities. The God of Islam and of Christianity—like the God of Judaism, which was the parent of both these creeds, —is "a living and a jealous God." He cannot tolerate any companion or sharer in the hearts of His adorers. Hence, the absorption of the Indo-Muslims into the fold of Hinduism by recognizing Allah as another of the numberless incarnations of Vishnu and Muhammad as an inspired sadhu, was impossible. Therefore, Hindus and Muhammadans, —as, later on, Hindus and Christians, —had to live in the same land without being able to mix together. Nothing has enabled them to bridge this gulf. The Indian Muslims have, throughout the succeeding centuries, retained the extra-Indian direction of their hearts. Their faces are still turned in daily prayer, to a spot in Mecca; their minds, their law-code, their administrative system, their favourite reading sought models from outside India, —from Arabia and Syria, Persia, and Egypt. All Muhammadans have the same sacred language literature and era, teachers, saints, and shrines, throughout the world, instead of these being restricted to India, as is the case with the Hindus.

The Hindus were willing to absorb the Muslims; they wrote the Allopanishad and went perilously near to making an avatar of the emperor Akbar. But the Muhammadans would not yield on the cardinal points of their faith, nor accept the few conventions necessary for entering Hindu society. They clung to the Quranic precepts: "The polytheists are unclean; let nothing unclean enter the Kaba."

This was the cardinal difference between the Muslim settlement in India and all the other foreign immigrations that had gone before it. Another equally important characteristic of the Muslim element in India was that from 1200 to 1580 their State and society retained its original military and nomadic character,—the ruling race living merely like an armed camp in the land. It was Akbar who, at the end of the sixteenth century, began the policy of giving to the people of the country an interest in the State and making the Government undertake some socialistic functions in addition to the mere police work it had hitherto contented itself with doing. Up to Akbar's time the Muslim settlers in India used to be in the land but not of it.

The gifts of the Muslim age to India.

What were the gifts of the Muslim age to India? They were the following ten:

i. Restoration of touch with the outer world, which included the revival of an Indian navy and sea-borne trade, both of which had been lost since the decline of the Cholas.
ii. Internal peace over a large part of India, especially north of the Vindhyas.
iii. Uniformity secured by the imposition of the same type of administration.
iv. Uniformity of social manners and dress among the upper classes, irrespective of creed.
v. Indo-Saracen art, in which the mediæval Hindu and Chinese schools were blended together. Also, a new style of architecture, and the promotion of industries of a refined kind (e.g., shawl, inlaying work, Kinkhab, muslin, carpet, &c.)

vi. A common lingua franca, called Hindustani or Rekhta, and an official prose style (mostly the creation of Hindu munshis writing Persian, and even borrowed by the Maratha chitnises for their own vernacular.)

vii. Rise of our vernacular literature, as the fruits of peace and economic prosperity under the empire of Delhi.

viii. Monotheistic religious revival and Sufism.

ix. Historical literature.

x. Improvements in the art of war and in civilization in general.

India's contact with the outer world re-established by Muhammadans.

The intimate contact between India and the outer Asiatic world which had been established in the early Buddhistic age was lost when the new Hindu society as reorganized and set in rigidity like a concrete structure about the eighth century A. D., with the result that India again became self-centred and isolated from the Loving world beyond her natural barriers.

This touch.with the rest of Asia and the nearest parts of Africa was restored by the Muslim conquest at the end of the 12th century but with a difference. The Hindus no longer went outside, as they had done in the Buddhistic age; only many thousands of foreigners poured into India and some Indian Muslims went abroad every year.

"Through the passes of the Afghan frontier the stream of population and trade flowed peacefully into India from Bukhara and Samarqand, Balkh and Khurasan, Khwarizm and Persia because Afghanistan belonged to the ruler of Delhi, till near the end of the Mughal empire (1739). Through the Bolan Pass, leading from India to Qandahar and Persia, as many as 14,000 camel-loads of merchandise passed every year in the reign of Jahangir, early in the 17th century. The ports on our western coast were so many doors between India and the outer world that could be reached by sea. From the eastern-port of Masulipatam, belonging to the Sultans of Golkonda up to 1687 and thereafter to the Mughals, —ships used to sail for Ceylon, Sumatra, Java, Siam and even China."*

* J. Sarkar's Mughal Administration 2nd. ed.,241

Uniformity of administration and cultured life.

"The two hundred years of Mughal rule gave to the whole of northern India and too much of the Deccan also, oneness of official language, administrative system and coinage and also a popular lingua franca for all classes except the Hindu priests and the stationary village folk. Even outside the territory directly administered by the Mughal emperors, their administrative system, official titles,

Court etiquette and monetary type were borrowed, more or less, by the neighbouring Hindu rajahs.

All the twenty Indian subahs of the Mughal empire were governed by means of exactly the same administrative machinery, with exactly the same procedure and official titles. Persian was the one language used in ail official records &c.... Officials and soldiers were frequently transferred from one province to another. Thus, the native of one province felt himself almost at home in another province; traders and travellers passed most easily from city to city, subah to subah and all realized the imperial oneness of this vast country."*

*Mughal Administrations, 238-239.

Muslim art: its nature.

In the domain of the fine arts, the richest contributions of the Muhammadans are a new style of architecture (especially palaces and tombs), the Indo-Saracen school of painting, and artificial gardening.

"In the earliest Muslim paintings to reach India, namely, those from Khurasan and Bukhara, we see complete Chinese influence, especially in representing the faces, rocks, sheets of water, fire and dragons....In the Court of our truly national king Akbar, this Chinese or extra-Indian Muslim art mingled with pure Hindu art—whose traditions had been handed down unchanged since the days of the Ajanta frescoes and the Bharhut and Ellora reliefs. Thus, Muslim art in India underwent its first transformation. The rigidity of the Chinese outline was softened. The conventionality of Chinese art was discarded. We note a new method of representing rocks, water, and fire, which is no doubt suggestive of the Chinese school, but it is clearly the Chinese school in a process of dissolution and making a nearer approach to Nature. The scenery and features are distinctly Indian....This process of the Indianization of Saracen art continued after Akbar's time, till at last in the reign of Shah Jahan, the Chinese influence entirely disappeared, the Indian style became predominant and the highest development was reached in delicacy of features and colouring, minuteness of detail, wealth and variety of ornamentation and approximation to Nature,—but without attaining either to true perspective or to light and shade. This Indo-Saracen art was entirely developed in the Courts of the Mughal emperors." Studies in Mughal India, 289-291.]

Thus, in painting there was a true revival and the highest genius was displayed by Indian artists in the Mughal age. This style lingers on in our times under the name of "Indian art" or "Mughal painting."

Growth of vernacular literatures.

In the history of Europe, we find that the social revolution caused by the Barbarian overthrow of the Roman empire continued through the Dark Ages till the 13th century, when the former provinces of the Roman empire re-appeared as independent national kingdoms and in each of them a vernacular literature sprang up, which took the place of the old common cultural language Latin. Chaucer (c. 1360), Dante (c. 1300) and the Troubadours (12th century) are the morning stars of song in the respective languages of England, Italy and France. In India, too, the old Sanskrit literature ceased to be a living growth after 1200 A.D. Though Sanskrit works continued to be written long after that date and have been written even in our own times, these are entirely artificial works, —mere, commentaries, or commentaries on commentaries, conventional treatises or tours de force, and not original productions deserving the name of literature. They fail to appeal to our hearts or to add to our stock of knowledge, so that, it may be truly said that what is popularly called the Pathan period, i.e., from 1200 to 1550, was the Dark Age of north Indian history and the Hindu intellect was barren during these three centuries and a half. But, by the time that Akbar had conquered his enemies and established a broad empire covering all northern India, —peace and good administration began to produce their natural fruits. With the feeling of security, wealth grew, and wealth brought leisure and a passion for the things of the mind. There was a sudden growth of vernacular literature in all our provinces. In Bengal a new impulse was given to the creative instinct by the followers of Chaitanya (1485-1533), who wrote the first great works—as distinct from folksongs, —in modern Bengali. Such were the saint's biographies, the Chaitanya Bhagavat (1573), the Chaitanya-charitamrita (completed 1582) and the two Chaitanya-mangals of Jayananda and Lochan Das (c. 1575) and the biographical and mystical works of the monks and their lay devotees.

In the Hindi-speaking world the greatest master was Tulsidas (born 1529), who began his immortal and perennially inspiring Rama-charit-manasa in 1574. He had been preceded by a Muslim poet, Malik Muhammad Jaisi, whose allegorical romance, the Padumavat had been completed in 1540 and Mrigavat in 1502. There was quite a crop of Hindi poems produced in this age such as the Akharavat, Sapanavat, Kandaravat, Madhu Malati, Usman's Chitravati (1613), Sura-sahitya-lahari (completed 1546) and Purushottam Vaishya's Dharmashwamedh (1501 A.D.)*

*I do not refer to eighteenth century or very late 17th century vernacular poetical romances like the Bengali works of Al Awal of Chittagong or Nur Muhammad's Hindi poem Indravati (1742).

I do not here refer to the Hindi religious poems of an earlier age, like those of Kabir (d. 1518) Dadu (c. 1600) and Nanak (1469-1538) because they were not literature proper but more in the nature of aphorisms intended to be committed to the memory and transmitted orally.

Nor do I refer to the Persian literature (other than history) produced in India under the patronage of Akbar and his successors because it was an exotic. Many of the Persian poets of the Delhi Court down to the middle of the 17th century were emigrants from Persia. Such were Muhammad Jan Qudsi (of Mashhad), Abu Talib (of Hamdan), Saida (of Gilan) and others of lesser note. Their productions have no life, no value as literature.

Urdu came into being in the 16th century but only as a vulgar spoken tongue, despised by authors and cultured society. It became a literary language in the North only in the late 18th century, Wali of Aurangabad (c. 1710) having been its first recognized poet of note. But the southern Urdu or Rekhta had produced good poetry a century before Wali.

The literary impulse given by the peace and prosperity of Akbar's long and successful reign and the patronage of that emperor, and his vassal princes led to a wonderful flowering of the Indian intellect at the close of the 16th and the first half of the 17th centuries. To this period belong the curious corrupt Sanskrit history of Bengal entitled Shaikh-subhodaya, the Persian writings of Chandrabhan Brahman, a courtier and diplomat of Shah Jahan, and other works of that type.

Monotheistic and anti-caste movements within Hinduism during Muslim rule.

Let us now consider the result of the impact of Islam—both creed and society—on the Hindus and the reaction of Islam, to its Hindu environment during the many centuries that these two faiths have lived together in the same land. Cunningham, the historian of the Sikhs, as early as the middle of the nineteenth century thus described the moral effect of the Muslim conquest:

"The influence of a new people, who equalled or surpassed Kshatriyas in valour, who despised the sanctity of Brahmans and who authoritatively proclaimed the unity of God and His abhorrence of images, —began gradually to operate on the minds of the-multitude of India. . . New superstition emulated old credulity. Pirs and shahids, saints and martyrs, equalled Krishna and Bhairav in the number of their miracles and the Muhammadans almost forgot the unity of God in the multitude of intercessors whose aid they implored."*

*History of the Sikhs 2nd ed., 30-31.

That was one effect, —the growth of popular superstition; but something higher soon followed. I quote Cunningham again:

"The first result of the conflict [between Hinduism and Islam] was the institution about the end of the 14th century of a comprehensive sect by Ramananda of Benares. . . He seized upon the idea of man's equality before God. He instituted no nice distinctive observances; he admitted all classes of people as his disciples.... About 1450, the mysterious (i.e., mystic) weaver Kabir assailed at once the worship of idols, the authority of the Quran and Shastras and the exclusive use of a learned language."

But it is historically incorrect to hold, as Hunter and some other European writers have done that the monotheistic and anti-caste movements among the Hindus in the Middle Ages originated in Islam. We know that all the higher thinkers, all the religions reformers, all the sincere devotees among the Hindus from the earliest times, have proclaimed one and only one supreme God behind the countless deities of popular worship and have declared the equality of all true adorers and placed a simple sincere faith above elaborate religious ceremonies; they have all tried to simplify religion and bring it to the doors of the commonest people. Hence, what really happened after the Muslim conquest was that these dissenting or reforming movements among the Hindus received a great impetus from the presence of the Muhammadans in their immediate neighbourhood. The example of Islamic society acted as a solvent on Hindu prejudice.

Many sects arose which tried to harmonize Islam and Hinduism and to afford a common meeting-ground to the devout men of both creeds, in which their differences of ritual, dogma and external marks of faith were ignored. This was the avowed aim of Kabir and Dadu, Nanak and Chaitanya. They made converts freely from Hindus and Muslims and rejected the rigid orthodoxy of the Brahman and the Mulla alike.

The Sufi brotherhood.

So, too, the Sufi movement afforded a common platform to the more learned and devout minds among the Hindus and Muhammadans. Unlike the abovementioned popular religions of mediæval India, Sufism never extended to the illiterate people. It was essentially a faith, —or rather an intellectual-emotional enjoyment—reserved for the philosophers, authors, and mystics free from bigotry. The eastern variety of Sufism is mainly an offshoot of the Vedanta of the Hindus and it rapidly spread and developed in India from the time of Akbar, under whose fostering care Hindu and Muslim thought formed a close union, with help from: many Persian emigrants of liberal views. Akbar's mantle as an eclectic and peacemaker in religion fell on his great-grandson Dara Shukoh, who openly declared that he had found the fullest pantheism (tauhid) in the Vedanta only and prepared a Persian translation of fifty of the Upanishads and another work bearing the significant title of Majmua-ul-baharain or 'the mingling of the two oceans', which explains for Persian readers the technical terms of Hindu pantheism, with their parallels in Sufi phraseology, in order to facilitate the study of the subject by members of both creeds.

In short, the popular religious sects founded by our medieval saints and the Sufi philosophy tended to bring the ruling race and the subject people closer together.

Another gift of the Muslims to India is historical literature. The chronological sense was very imperfectly developed among the Hindus, who are apt to despise this world and its ephemeral occurrences. Before the Islamic conquest, they produced no true history at all. On the other hand, the Arab intellect is dry, methodical and matter of fact. All their records contain a chronological framework. The historical literature of the Muhammadans in all countries has been vast and varied and well furnished with dates. We therein get a solid basis for historical study. The Persian chronicles which were written under every Muslim dynasty in India and in every reign under the Mughals, not only served as materials of study in themselves but furnished an example which Hindu writers and Hindu rulers were not slow to imitate. Thus, a new and very useful element was introduced into Indian literature and in the 17th and 18th centuries it formed a magnificent body, —if we take all the histories biographies and letters into account.

Other examples of Muslim influence still surviving.

The cultural influence of the six centuries of Muslim rule was necessarily wide-spread. Hunting, hawking and many games became Muhammadanized in method and terminology. In other departments also, Persian, Arabic and Turkish words have entered largely into the Hindi, Bengali and even Marathi languages. The art of war was very highly developed by the Muslims, partly by borrowing from Europe through Turkey and to a lesser extent through Persia. The imperial Mughal army served as a model which Hindu rajahs eagerly imitated.

The system of fortification was greatly improved by the Muhammadans in India, as a natural consequence of the general advance of civilization and the introduction of artillery.

The Muslim influence was naturally most strongly felt on the system of administration, the Court ceremonials and dress, the military organization and arms, the lives of the upper classes, the articles of luxury, fine arts, architecture (other than religious) and gardening. In Court life and even the titles and office procedure of State officials, the Mughal empire set the fashion which the Hindu rajahs often slavishly copied. In some Rajput and Malwa Hindu States, the official language even today is Urdu, and the Persian script is used instead of Devanagari.

The basis of the revenue system was indigenous and a continuation of the village organization that had come down from before recorded history, but the official arrangements, titles and method of record-keeping were due to the Perso-Saracen model imported by the Muslim invaders, and these were borrowed by the Hindu States. [Mughal Administration, 2nd ed, ch. 5 and 11.]

In warfare, gunpowder was introduced and cavalry rose to great prominence eclipsing the elephants of the old Hindu days. This animal now ceased to be an arm and. continued as a mere transport agency.

The Muslims, leading generally a more luxurious life than the Hindus and being a predominantly city population (except in East Bengal), encouraged several manufactures and fine arts. They were more tasteful and elegant than the Hindus in their daily life and even in their vices, —which the richer Hindus and particularly the official class copied whenever they had the means. By the agency of the Muhammadans, new articles of food and new styles of cookery were introduced. In aesthetics, perfumery and—though not so completely, in music and dancing also, —the Muslim royal family guided the taste of the entire Indian society.

Paper was introduced by the Muhammadans, as the Arabic word kaghaz proves. Thus, books could be multiplied in a more attractive and durable form than by scratching on palm leaves. The illumination of manunscripts is an art which we owe to the Mughal empire and from Akbar's time onwards Hindi and Sanskrit works were finely copied and illustrated for the sake of Hindu rajahs, while the Persian book illumination and calligraphy then done in India enjoys deserved fame in Europe. We owe to the Muhammadan influence the practice of diffusing knowledge by the copying and circulation of books, while the earlier Hindu writers, as a general rule, loved to make a secret of their productions.

The best medical men of the age were the Yunani hakims or Muslim physicians practising the Græco-Arab system of medicine. This was due partly to the patronage of the Court and of the nobility but mainly to the fact that the progress of Hindu medicine had been arrested long ago, while Muslim medical science was daily progressing by keeping touch with the West.

The Muhammadans were the only foreign traders of India (if we leave out the European sojourners in the land). This naturally resulted in a greater expansion of their minds in comparison with those of the stay-at-home Hindus. In the Persian language, a travelled man, mard-i-jihan-dida, is rightly considered as a model of wisdom and culture.

V

THE ENGEISH AND THEIR GIFTS TO INDIA

The Portuguese were the first among the Europeans to settle in India. They have enriched Indian vocabulary and medical science to some extent; their descendants (usually of mixed breed) have spread through all the provinces of India and were a noticeable element of the population in the Mughal age. But the Portuguese as rulers created a strong feeling of repulsion in the Indian mind, by their cruelty, their religious bigotry such as the conversion of the temples of Shanti-Durga into Christian churches, — their establishment of the Inquisition at Goa, and their rapid moral decline. The Indian territory under their rule was very small in area and situated in an obscure and rather inaccessible corner of the peninsula. Hence the influence of the Portuguese on Indian life and thought has been negligible.

How the European newcomers differ from the Aryan and Muslim settlers of old.

The modernization of India is the work of the English, and it has affected the entire Indian continent.

The Europeans have struck the undefended sea-board of India. The sole condition of their power is naval supremacy, and their hold on India can be maintained only by a regular flow of reinforcements from their distant homeland in every generation. Thus, unlike the Indo-Greeks, Indo-Parthians, Scythians, Pathans and Mughals, the English have not made India their home, they must ever be sojourners in this land and keep up a constant intercourse with their European home, in the form of the double stream of incoming recruits and home-returning pensioners. Their rise and fall depend not on what happens in India but on the military and political position of their mother country, which is the central powerhouse of their far-flung empire.

In many respects the English have continued, but in a more thorough fashion and over a much wider area of India, the work begun by the Mughal empire and in some others, they have introduced new forces which were unknown in the Mughal age. The English influence on Indian life and thought, which is still working and still very far from its completion, is comparable only to the ancient Aryan stimulus, in its intensity and its all-pervasive character.

The gifts of the English.

i. The first gift of the English to India is universal peace, or freedom from foreign invasion and internal disorder. How valuable peace is for national growth can be best understood by contrast if we study the history of Western India before 1817 or of the Panjab in the 18th century. The British Indian empire embraces the whole of India as well as the neighbouring lands east and west of it. A peace so profound and spread over such an extensive territory, had never before been seen in India. The English have completed and carried to perfection the task undertaken by Akbar but reversed by the anarchy that followed the dissolution of the Mughal empire after Nadir Shah's invasion.

ii. Secondly, the English have restored our contact with the outer world. The Mughals had opened communication by sea with Persia and Arabia, Zanzibar and the Abyssinian coast, the Malay Peninsula and Java, and by land with Central Asia. But even this limited range of intercourse had been interrupted by the decline of the Mughal empire, when Persia and Arabia, Bukhara and Khurasan ceased to send their adventurers and traders to India

The English have admitted us to the entire outside world, —not only in Asia, but in all other continents as well, —and they have admitted the rest of the world to us, in a degree not dreamt of under Muslim rule. India has now been switched on to the main currents of the great moving world outside, and made to vibrate with every economic or cultural change there. An isolated life is no longer possible even for our remotest villages. A medicinal discovery in Paris or Toronto becomes available in India in two months. A poor harvest in Poland or Canada makes people in Lyallpur starve by sending up the price of wheat. A careless engine-driver causes a cotton blaze in Texas, and the result is that hillmen in Almora and Assam suffer from cold because of the increased price of clothing. The telegraph, railway and newspapers have completed the suction of India into the whirlpool of world movements of every kind. We cannot now sit down self-contained, secluded within our natural barriers.

iii. And not only have these modern agencies connected us with the outer world more extensively and fully than ever before but coupled with the uniformity of administrative system which is a gift of the British age, they have also been tending to fuse the various races and creeds of India into one homogeneous people and to bring about social equality and community of life and thought, which are the necessary basis of nationality. The process has Just begun, though its completion is yet far off.

The new spirit of progress, opposed to Oriental passivity and fatalism.

iv. Fourthly, the direct action of the State and even more than that the indirect example of the English people, have infused a spirit of progress into the Indians. Our best thinkers are no longer content with adoring the wisdom of our Vedic ancestors, they feel an eternal discontent with things as they are and translate that discontent into action by trying to make our State and religion, education and industry, life and thought, better and still better. Our most effective leaders do not repeat the pessimism of pre-British days by despising the moderns as a race of degenerate pigmies and sighing for the return of the golden age of the far-off past (Satya Yuga). Their gaze is fixed forward. We have now accepted the principle of progress in practice, even when we profess on our lips to reject it and worship our old indigenous institutions and ideas.

One effect of this attitude of mind on the part of our rulers and wiser leaders is the increased efficiency and purity of the administration and the various agencies of social service, by conscious persistent effort. To take one instance only, official bribery was admitted to be an immoral thing even in Mughal times, and yet almost all the officials practised it, and no edict of the emperor could stop it. The English in the days of Warren Hastings and Cornwallis, took over the rotten remnant of the- Mughal administration, and set about reforming it. Their strength lay not only in the solid phalanx of absolutely honest and dependable English officers (after deducting a small number of corrupt or weak ones), —but also in their perseverance and activity, their long-thought out plans and ceaseless continuity of exertion for purifying the administration. The removal of this abuse has been possible because it has not been dependent on the personality of this governor or that but has been adopted as the policy and pursued as a generally desired thing by the entire European society in India, —both official and nonofficial. The public have cordially helped the State in purifying the administration.

In fact, modern European civilization contains within itself a spirit of self-criticism and a perennial desire for reform by voluntary effort. The shock of foreign conquest or the screed of a foreign prophet is not required to waken the nation to a sense of the moral canker that is eating into its vitals. The people are too self-conscious to forget the malady in their body politic. It is daily proclaimed to them from the Press and the pulpit.

The Renaissance in modern India.

v. The greatest gift of the English, after universal peace and the modernization of society, and indeed the direct result of these two forces, —is the Renaissance which marked our 19th century. Modern India owes everything to it. This Renaissance was at first an intellectual awakening and influenced our literature, education, thought and art but in the next generation it became a moral force and reformed our society and religion. Still later, in the third generation from its commencement, it has led to the beginning of the economic modernization of India.

The old order was dead when the English conquest began.

When the English power first asserted itself in India in the middle of the 18th century, the country had reached the lowest point of moral decay and political weakness. Northern India had enjoyed a fairly long spell of peace and growth of wealth during the 160 years of stable rule under the Mughal emperors from 1570 to 1730. But thereafter material prosperity had been destroyed, the population thinned, trade and communication interrupted, and culture thrown backwards, by incessant warfare among small States, or between rival claimants to the throne, and the incursions of predatory bands that took advantage of the anarchy and administrative weakness following the eclipse of the great empire of Delhi. Over the Mysore plateau and the Madras Karnatak, the fall of the Vijaynagar empire (1565) had let loose the dogs of civil war and rapine. After 1687, the dissolution of the sultanates of Bijapur and Golkonda—which had maintained peace and order in these parts for about a hundred years—left this country a prey to four sets of contending but weak authorities,—the representatives of the old Hindu rulers, the now masterless vassals and captains of Bijapur and Golkonda, the Mughal conqueror (who claimed to be their heir-at-law) and the Maratha intruders. The economic desolation caused by these forces is graphically described in the old records of the English Factory at Madras and the memoirs of Francois Martin, the founder of Pondicherry.*

* Sarkar's History of Aurangzib, vol. v. ch. 51 §4, 8, &c.

In the next century, i.e., the eighteenth, began the succession wars in the families of the Nizam and the Nawab of Arcot, which ravaged this unhappy land for a generation.

On the western side of the Deccan, the downfall first of the Bahmani empire (c. 1526) and then of its successor the monarchy of Ahmadnagar (c. 1600), caused local aspirants to kingship to fight out their ceaseless wars of ambition throughout the first half of the 17th century, while in the second half of that century, the rise of the Marathas and then the Mughal-Maratha struggle denied peace and quiet to the troubled country till the rise of the Peshwas (c. 1730).

Northern India became a scene of plunder and slaughter† after the death of the Emperor Muhammad Shah (1748), and this anarchy ceased only with Lord Lake's victorious entrance into Delhi in 1803.

† Singh gardi, Shah gardi and Bhau-gardi are the three classes of raid and slaughter still remembered with terror by old men in the Upper Provinces. They refer to the Sikh the Abdali and the Maratha incursions in the second half of the 18th century.

Bengal had greatly prospered under the Mughal peace from the reign of Jahangir (when the last remnant of Pathan power and the refractory independent zamindars were crushed by the Delhi forces) to the battle of Plassey (1757). But that battle had encouraged up-country robber-bands, calling themselves Sannyasis or faqirs, to flock to the province which was supposed to be masterless after the fall of its old Nawabs. It taxed all the energy and organizing genius of Warren Hastings to stamp out the Sannyasi pest, but he succeeded in the end.

In fact, the unsettled condition of the country and the decay of normal civilized life among the people can be best judged from the fact that just before Wellesley imposed British suzerainty over the country, i.e., at the end of the 18th century, there were a million mercenary soldiers seeking employment at any Indian Court that would hire them. These men had no loyalty, no local patriotism, no discipline. The ruin of agriculture and trade over most parts of India as the result of the disintegration of the Mughal empire, drove all strong and ambitious men to seek their livelihood by flocking to the profession of soldiers of fortune or of robbers.

Thus, it happened that in the middle years of the 18th century, Mughal civilization which had done so much good to India from the reign of Akbar to that of Aurangzib, was like a spent bullet; all its life and vigour were gone. This rottenness at the core of Indian society first made itself felt in the form of military and political weakness. The country could not defend itself; royalty was hopelessly depraved and imbecile; the nobles were selfish and short-sighted; corruption, inefficiency and treachery disgraced all branches of the public service.

In the midst of this decay and confusion, our literature art and even true religion perished.

Destruction of the old order under Hastings and Cornwallis a necessary preliminary to the birth of a new India under Bentinck and Hardinge.

Just at this time the West struck India with irresistible impact, though its full force was concealed for some half-a-century, namely, the period from Clive to Cornwallis. Then followed what we may call "the dark age of modern India", the period extending from Cornwallis to Bentinck (or roughly 1790 to 1830), during which the old order was dead, but the new had not yet begun, and nobody could foresee what shape the life and thought of India to come would take.

In the interests of efficiency and public good, the Indians were totally excluded from the public service, the command of the army and the control of education.* The future seemed hopelessly dark to the great-grandsons of Aurangzib's generals and ministers, poets and scholars, who found themselves reduced to obscurity and unemployment in the early British administration.

*'The system established by Lord Cornwallis was based upon the principle of doing everything by European agency— The plan which Lord William Bentinck substituted for this was to transact the public business by native agency under European superintendence" (Trevelyan's Education & c.)

But the destruction of the old order which took place under Warren Hastings and Cornwallis was a necessary process before the new order could come into being. It was a painful but indispensable operation, like the burning of the stubble on the reaped field, as a preparation for the next crop. To the English destroyer of the old order in India we might truly apply the words of Kalidas:

"Holy father! this curse of yours is to me really a blessing in disguise. When the fire burns a cultivated field, it makes it the more fertile for sending up shoots from the seeds sown." [Raghuvamsam, ix. 80.]

I therefore prefer to call it the "seed time of New India," rather than the dark age of modern India.

At the end of this period, i.e., in Lord William Bentinck's time, we find Indians again beginning to take an honourable and responsible part in guiding their countrymen's thoughts, shaping the national life, and conducting the country's government. But these were Indians of a new breed; they drew their inspiration and their strength not from the East but from the West. They had acquired English learning and had thus properly equipped themselves for the work of the modern age. They were the first fruits of the Indian Renaissance and their prophet was Ram Mohan Roy, whose life (1774-1833) exactly bridges this dark age in the history of modern India.

The beginnings of the Indian Renaissance: Passion for English education in Bengal.

The history of the Indian Renaissance is profoundly interesting and deserves a detailed treatment. It began with our study of English literature and modern philosophy and science from books written in the English language. Rajah Ram Mohan Roy was the first Indian to write books in English and he visited England. The beginnings of English education can be traced even earlier than his time, but the knowledge of English acquired by his predecessors, whether in Bengal or in Madras, —was limited to the requirements of clerks and interpreters serving English masters, it was not pursued as an instrument of culture by our entire literate class. As early as 1789 we find an appeal published in a Calcutta paper by several Bengali gentlemen inviting some European to write a grammar of the English language for the benefit of the Bengali people.*

* "We humbly beseech any gentleman will be so good to us as to take the trouble of making a Bengali Grammar and Dictionary, in which we hope to find all the common Bengali country words made into English. By this means we shall be enabled to recommend ourselves to the English Government and understand their orders; this favour will be gratefully remembered by us and our posterity for ever." (23rd April 1789. Selections from the Calcutta Gazette, ii. 497.)

But from 1810 onwards we find English education, at first of the school standard, spreading throughout Bengal, thanks to the efforts of the Christian missions. Two external causes contributed to this development of schools:

i. Lord Wellesley's conquests not only established British paramountcy and gave internal peace to India but extended the English dominion throughout that ancient home of civilization, the Gangetic valley up to Delhi.
ii. The missionaries were allowed by the Charter Act of 1813 to carry on their propaganda in British territory instead of being confined to the Danish settlement of Serampur, as they had been before this by the orders of Barlow and Minto.

The College of Fort William, which the far-sighted Wellesley had founded in 1800, though it was soon afterwards starved and curtailed, worked for English education, by bringing European officer-students and Indian teachers together, and compelling each to learn the language of the other. This college, however, did not tend to diffuse the knowledge of English among our countrymen in general. Up to Lord William Bentinck's time (1835) it was held by Government that European philosophy and science should be taught to the Indians by translation into Sanskrit and Arabic and not through the medium of English.

Early English schools established by the people and Christian Missionaries and piled with pupils.

But long before that date the people had taken their destiny into their own hands and begun to flock to the English schools started by the missionaries and by a few enlightened Indians. English education was not a gift of the E. I. Company's Government, though some financial aid was given to it by the State from 1835 onwards. Previous to that date* all the expenses of the schools had been borne by the pupils, the missionaries or Indian donors and English subscribers. As late as 1850, nearly 47 p. c. of the total educational expenditure in Bengal was met from the pupils' fees and private subscriptions.

*There was one exception. The General Committee of Public Instruction, constituted in 1823, undertook "to take under their patronage and greatly improve the Hindu College at Calcutta, which had been founded as far back as 1816, by the voluntary contributions of the natives themselves for the instruction of their youth in English literature and science.'' English classes were afterwards established in connection with the Muhammadan and Sanskrit Colleges at Calcutta (1827), the Sanskrit College at Benares and the Agra College (1832) and a separate institution was founded at Delhi in 1829 for the cultivation of western learning (Trevelyan, 3-4). The Scottish missionary, Br. Duff, opened his college in Calcutta in 1830.

The passion of young Bengal to study English literature, even before Lord William Bentinck opened the subordinate Judicial service to them by Regulation V of 1831, is well illustrated by Sir Charles Trevelyan: —

"On the opening of the Hughli College, in August 1886, students of English flocked to it in such numbers as to render the organization and classification of them a matter of difficulty. Twelve hundred names were entered on the books of this department of the college within three days....There appears to be no limit to the number of scholars, except that of the number of teachers whom the Committee [of Public Instruction] is able to provide. Notwithstanding the extraordinary concourse of English students at Hughli, the demand was so little exhausted that when an auxiliary school was lately opened within two miles of the college, the English department of it was instantly filled and numerous applicants were sent away unsatisfied." [On the Education of the People of India, 1836, p. 82.]

He continues: "The curiosity of the people is thoroughly roused and the passion for English knowledge has penetrated the most obscure and extended to the most remote parts of India. The steamboats, passing up and down the Ganges are boarded by native boys, begging not for money but for books...... Some English gentlemen coming to Calcutta were astonished at the eagerness with which they were pressed for books by a troop of boys, who boarded the steamer from an obscure place called Kumarkhali [120 miles north of Calcutta] ......The gentleman at last hit upon the expedient of cutting up an old Quarterly Review and distributing the articles among them." (P. 167).

From 1835, when Government adopted the policy of giving State aid and supervision to schools teaching English, in preference to those teaching Oriental classical languages, English schools multiplied very quickly, and their number was trebled in Bengal in the next five years (1836-40). Another impetus was given to the movement by Sir Henry Hardinge, who, on 10th October 1844, issued a resolution announcing that in future preference would be given, in first appointments, to candidates educated in the Government English schools. Ten years rolled by and then our educational edifice was crowned by the establishment of a university on the model of the London University in each of our three Presidencies, —as ordered in Sir Charles Wood's Despatch of 1854 and passed by legislation in 1857.

VI

THE RENAISSANCE IN BRITISH INDIA AND ITS EFFECT

The marvellous transformation and modernization of our vernacular literatures: its stages.

The first effect of the Indian Renaissance was felt in our vernacular literatures, which have undergone a complete change and at the same time approximated to one parent standard, namely, English literature. The work of centuries has been crowded into a few decades in this evolution of our modern literatures. My illustrations are all taken from Bengal.

The first generation of Indians educated in English accepted European literature philosophy and history and to a lesser extent science, —with enthusiasm and tried to diffuse them among their countrymen by translation, while attempting little or no original composition of their own. They did not display any literary genius except in manipulating the language for a new need. To this earliest generation belonged Krishna Mohan Banerji (1813-1885), Rajendra Lala Mitra (1821-1892), Peary Chand Mitra (1815-1883) and Pandit Ishwar Chandra Vidyasagar (1820-1891). They wrote translations, adaptations and epitomes of English works and did not create any revolution in Bengali thought or style.

A little later came another group of authors, who introduced the new order in its full majesty. They were Michael Madhusudan Dutt the poet (1824-1873), Dinabandhu Mitra the dramatist (1830-1874) and Bankim Chandra Chatterji the novelist (1838-1894)—each of whom reigned over one branch of literature and turned it into a new channel, where it has since flowed at his bidding. Their work has been continued by their successors, notably by Hem Chandra Banerji (1838-1902), Nabin Chandra Sen (1847-1909) and Rabindra Nath Tagore (b. 1862). In their writings the influence of English literature is unmistakable but equally unmistakable is their success in adapting the foreign spirit and literary model (and even technique) to the Indian-mind and tradition. The best specimens of this new vernacular literature are European in spirit, in outlook, in literary devices, in the choice and treatment of subjects but they retain a close connection with the best in the literature and life of ancient India. They represent the spirit of England clad in a half oriental garb. There has been no wholesale borrowing but an assimilation of foreign models, while retaining a surprising amount of originality.

How the style has been changed.

Our vernacular languages have been wonderfully developed and, in some cases, almost revolutionized by the example of English style and the needs of the modern world. Our literary language has become both simpler and harder at the same time. It has acquired an unwonted flexibility, variety and naturalness of movement, while the vocabulary has been greatly amplified. Madhusudan Dutt and Ishwar Chandra Vidyasagar, (middle 19th century), greatly modernized the Bengali tongue and made it a proper vehicle for expressing the varied thoughts and feelings of the present day. Both followed the classical style, i.e., they used Sanskrit words by preference and avoided colloquial or homely expressions. But at the same time there is no stiffness, no pedantry, no obscurity in their style and their genius was shown in combining clearness, sweetness, and beauty of expression with strength and purity of diction and a certain music of sound. The Indian drama has been completely transformed since the middle of the 19th century and is now really a close imitation of the modern European drama. Our greatest divergences from our older literature have been in the departments of the drama and the novel, in which we have been wholesale borrowers from the West. And this has been the case in every Indian vernacular.

The influence of Europe has also enriched our literature by kindling the patriotic spirit and developing a regard for our historic past. This awakened sense of nationality has added a manly and noble element to the Indian literature of our day. Here the Tagore's showed the way.

The net result of this literary revolution has been that the best pieces of modern Indian literature do not appear foreign or grotesque to European readers, as they really approximate to the spirit of Europe in plot, ill treatment of the subject and in the general characteristics of style.

Then, again, in the 19th century, we recovered our long-lost ancient literatures, Vedic and Buddhistic, as well as the buried architectural monuments of the Hindu days. The Vedas and their commentaries had totally disappeared from the plains of Aryavarta (Northern India), where none could interpret them, none had even a manuscript of the text. The English printed this ancient Scripture of the Indo-Aryans and brought it to our doors. A similar restoration of the ancient literature of Buddhism to the land of its origin has taken place through the enterprise and scholarship of Europeans. From Nepal, China and Japan Englishmen have sent the lost Buddhistic works to Europe and Europe has printed them and made them available to us.

But the mere study of a foreign or long-lost literature does not constitute a Renaissance. There must be a new birth of the spirit, there must be reforms in society religion and morals, following the intellectual awakening, before we can truly call the movement a Renaissance.

Social reform an effect of the Indian Renaissance.

As surely as the Renaissance in Europe was followed by the Reformation, so in India to a modification of our social relations, our general outlook upon life, our religious doctrines and practices was bound to result from the action of English education. Attempts at Hindu social reform began to take shape from 1855, under Pandit Ishwar Chandra Vidyasagar (1820-1891) who fought for and obtained legal sanction to the marriage of Hindu widows (1856) and tried (though without success) to forbid polygamy. Schools for Hindu girls began to be founded at this time, the Christian missionaries having opened schools for their converts' daughters 30 or 35 years earlier. But social reform received its greatest impetus and spread outside Calcutta to the country districts after the Sepoy Mutiny, from the personal magnetism and organizing genius of Keshav Chandra Sen (1838-1884). In addition to spreading female education and widow marriage, he organized temperance associations, night-schools, "uplift work" for the lower classes, inter-caste marriages, the creation and diffusion of cheap and pure popular literature, famine relief and other forms of social service. In Bengal, the most conspicuous followers in the path thus marked out were Shiva Nath Shastri (1847-1919) and Anand Mohan Bose (1847-1906).

The Reform movement in England which drew its inspiration from Bentham and Mill, and which began to bear fruit from 1832 onwards, first made itself felt among the Indian people about 25 years later as was until recently the case with all our borrowings from Europe. In England it was dissociated from religion, but the Indian movement went hand in hand with religious reform and was the direct offspring of the latter force.

The Renaissance continued unchecked and in full swing for more than one generation crowded with events and everything old or purely indigenous seemed to go down before it. But the very completeness of its victory led to a reaction in favour of orthodoxy, which was as curious in its nature as it was grotesque in its garb. At the first flush of the Renaissance, our ardent youths had been drawn to

Christianity, because the inner spirit of Hinduism had never been taught to them and they could find nothing but unreason and repulsiveness in the externals of Hinduism as practised in their day. To them the reform of such a religion seemed an impossibility. This explains the conversion to Christianity of Krishna Mohan Banerji (1813-1885), Lal Behari De (1826-1894), Govinda Dutt (the father of the poetess Torn Dutt) and several other highly educated Bengalis of the pre-Mutiny days. Others remained in the fold of Hindu society but with hardly concealed scepticism about its faith and practices.

The Brahmo Samaj: its internal history and achievement.

Then the Brahmo Samaj—which, first founded in 1828, had remained dead or somnolent for twenty-five years, was revived by Devendra Nath Tagore (1818-1905) and began an active propaganda in and outside Calcutta under the leadership of young Keshav Chandra Sen about 1860. Its intellectual appeal, refined spirituality and active social service brought many converts to it. The purely philosophical and aristocratic section of the educated Bengalis were attracted to the Adi Brahmo Samaj under Devendra Nath Tagore.

Thus, Brahmoism rose up to arrest the conversion of educated Hindus to Christianity. But Brahmoism proved only a halting place for the straying Hindus of the new school. Hinduism again asserted its marvellous assimilative power and changed its colour like the chameleon. Internal reforms were carried out and age-old abuses were removed in Hindu society, silently under the pressure of public opinion on the part of the rapidly increasing educated Hindu population. And then, early in the eighties of the 19th century began the modern Hindu revival. Champions sprang up to defend its philosophy and ritual and proclaim them to the world as the perfection of human thought!

The Hindu revival.

An "aggressive" Hinduism replaced the shy passive creed that used formerly to be ashamed of itself and to stand ever on the defensive against growing foes and a diminishing number of adherents. The conversion of educated Hindus even to Brahmoism ceased. The first philosophical exponents of this new or aggressive Hinduism in Bengal were Pandit Sasadhar Tarka-churamani (c. 1840-1928) and Bankim Chandra Chatterji. The former called science to his aid to prove that Hindu religions practices surcharged the body with electricity from the atmosphere and the earth. It was pseudo-science, no doubt but his audience knew no better science. He proved to his own satisfaction and to the exultation of his half-educated audience that the perfect development of a man's mind and body is possible in India only because here the succession of seasons is so regular, the climate is so free from extremes, the land is so fertile and well-watered. There are, he held, two opposite currents of electricity, one upward and one downward, through the universe, and the tuft of long hair at the back of the orthodox Hindu's head enables him to purify and invigorate his mind by helping the passage of these electrical currents through his body, for had not his hearers seen a horse-hair brush used for carrying away electricity in laboratory experiments? Therefore, all other religions and civilizations were defective, unscientific, and harmful in comparison with Hinduism.

These theories may raise a smile today, but their effect was extraordinary. The pandit had no natural gift of eloquence or charm of voice, his subject was new and not yet popular or familiar. But hundreds of clerks, schoolmasters, compositors and even shop assistants, on the way back from their places of business after a hard day's toil, would cheerfully stop in his lecture hall in the evening and listen spell-bound to Sasadhar for hours together. Soon the movement spread from the capital of Bengal to the district towns and everywhere a new Hindu organization raised its head. Touring preachers completed the work and one of them Srikrishna Prasanna Sen, added an emotional appeal and an eloquence which carried everything before them, while Pandit Shiva Chandra Vidyarnava made the deepest impression by his high Sanskrit scholarship, original thinking, and refined oratory.

The same effect was produced among the richer and better educated classes of Hindus by Bankim Chandra's defence of the cult of Krishna as a praiseworthy and quite natural form of hero-worship and his reply to the Christian polemic literature of the Rev. Dr. W. Hastie and K. S. Macdonald.

New Hinduism undertakes the service of man.

At a still later stage, in the closing decade of the 19th century, even the service of mankind (regardless of caste or creed) ceased to be an exclusive distinction of the Christian and Brahmo churches. At the trumpet call of Swami Vivekananda (1863-1902), the wealth and manhood of Hindu India rose to the need of the day and absorbed this form of moral activity, as more than a thousand years earlier Vaishnavism had risen to absorb the socialistic features of Mahayan Buddhism. The immense size of Hindu society and the newly acquired facility for forming organizations embracing the whole of India, almost completely took the wind out of the sails of the Christian and Brahmo churches, whenever public calamities called for voluntary relief-workers. This neo-Hinduism is clearly a fruit of the English Renaissance, working in an unexpected direction. Miss Margaret Noble, who entered Vivekananda's order under the name of Sister Nivedita, (1900-1913), most vigorously and eloquently carried on the intellectual propaganda of this "Aggressive Hinduism" and succeeded in kindling among us a new sense of the aesthetic aspects of Hindu art, Hindu domestic life, Hindu folktales, and Hindu ritual by her wonderful power of sympathy and delicate interpretation.

Earlier than Vivekananda, but in another part of India, Swami Dayananda (1827-1883) had started the Arya Samaj, which aimed at taking Hinduism back to what he understood to be the pristine purity of the Vedic age. Opinion will differ as to the spiritual value of his dogmatic creed and the philological correctness of his translation of the Rig Veda (Satyartha Prakas) but there cannot be two opinions as to the energy, spirit of progress and philanthropy that he succeeded in infusing among his followers, who now number several hundred thousands, and whose devotion to the service of suffering humanity extorts the admiration and emulation even of their opponents.

Rabindra Nath Tagore's "World Mission of India."

The latest form of the Hindu revival we owe to Rabindra Nath Tagore. It is a very close but unconscious copy of the movement which began in Russia in the 19th century, —the very language of the Slavonic leaders being repeated by the Indian poet. Its aim is exactly expressed if we replace the word Russia by India in the following descriptions of the movement in the former country:

Peter J. Chaadaev (b. at Moscow, 1793), wrote, "What use is it to seek culture among the people of the West? Have we not the beginning of a social structure superior to that of the West? Why should we envy the West, with its religious wars, its feudal system, its chivalry, its inquisition? Is the West, forsooth, the birth-place of Art and of all spiritual things? No, as you know, it is the East, —the East which we touch, from which we received our beliefs, laws and virtues, everything that has made us mighty.

"We belong to those nations which do not seem to form an integral part of humanity but exist in order to give some great lesson to the world. The lesson which we are destined to give will assuredly not be lost.

"The East and West must no longer remain apart from one another. Their diverse cultures must be synthetized in a new culture. It is Russia's mission to bring about this millennial synthesis, not by force but by means of a new social system or church, which will be the beginning of a universal Kingdom of Truth. In obedience to the will of God, Russia has to give the world new interpretations, a new message, a new example.

"Russia's gospel of resignation and humility, her asceticism, even her abstention from social activity, (seemed to him) notes of a Christianity purer than that of the West." (Quoted from C. H. Wright in the Fortnightly Review.)

"Like the Slavophils, Chernyshevsky wished to preserve the primitive socialism of the village commune, but he looked forward to a Russia which, by a chance of history, should escape the capitalist stage of modern Europe and achieve its development in accordance with the theories of modern socialism." "To the struggle for existence, Mikhailovsky opposes the struggle for individual completeness, which, he says, involves the fullest sense of the world around us." [Cambridge Modern History, xii. 296, 302.]

This latest form of Indian thought is based entirely on a new interpretation of our ancient Upanishads under the unconscious influence of Christianity. It is incorrect to call it a Hindu revival. It is really a cosmopolitan movement which aims at bringing all humanity together and hence the Eastern poet's appeal has found a response in some of the noblest hearts of the West.

History of political agitation in Modern-India.

The pioneers of political agitation in British India were the non-official Europeans who used to criticise the measures of Government rather virulently in their newspapers. The Press was placed under severe restraint by the E. I. Co.* and four English editors were deported from India by the Governors-General (1794, 1803 and 1823) for their objectionable writings. There were restrictions also on "interlopers" or European outsiders living and owning property in British India. These Europeans began an agitation in Calcutta in 1832, on the eve of the renewal of the E. I. Co.'s charter, protesting against the Company's monopoly of trade and autocratic government. But all this concerned the Europeans only, because the Indians, at this time had no newspaper of their own in the English language, while their vernacular papers were merely literary journals without any tinge of politics.

* Regulations of 1823 in Bengal and of 1825 and 1827 in Bombay. Sir Charles Metcalfe gave freedom to the Press in India in September 1835.

But the example set by the Calcutta Europeans was not lost upon the rising generation of English-educated Bengalis and their first appearance in the political field was under the wings of non-official English agitators. In 1842 Mr. George Thomson, M.P., came to Calcutta in the company of Dwarkanath Tagore. He discussed the political condition and problems of India with a number of well-to-do educated youths and delivered some inspiring speeches in public. The result was the foundation of the first political league of the Indians, viz., the British Indian Association, in 1851.

But public agitation by the Indians first took a perceptible form in 1853 when the E. I, Co.'s charter was going to be renewed by Parliament. This opportunity was seized to press for political rights for the Indian people too. Our first political orator was Ram Gopal Ghosh (1815-1868) and our first newspaper in English was the Hindoo Patriot, started in 1853 by Girish Chandra Ghosh (1829-1869)* who was later assisted and succeeded by Harish Chandra Mukherji, (1824-1861.)

*Girish and his brother had started the Bengal Recorder in 1851 but it ceased publication next year.

But these newspapers were confined to Calcutta and had the most limited circle of readers. Their publication was irregular and their owners lost heavily on the ventures. Ram Gopal Ghosh and his followers delivered academic speeches, painfully modelled on the British Eloquence, on a few set occasions. They reached only very small audiences—the only educated public of that day, —and produced a little intellectual stir without the least influence on public opinion or the march of events.

Just after the Sepoy Mutiny came the rising of the Bengal peasants against the European indigo planters (1860-62). Here European missionaries and officials (like the Rev. James Long and Ashley Eden) and Indian publicists (notably Harish Chandra Mukherji) joined hands and succeeded in putting an end to the oppression.

The next expansion of our political, agitation was due to Krishna Das Pal (1838-1884) and M. G. Ranade (1842-1901) but even their appeal did not go beyond the small educated upper middle class. At this stage its only method was the delivery of grave methodical speeches and the presentation of formal petitions to Government. Agitation became a living force for the first-time during Lord Lytton's viceroyalty (1876-1879), thanks to the efforts of Sisir Kumar Ghosh (1842-1911) and his brothers, who founded the Amrita Bazar Patrika, as a democratic rival to the staid and aristocratic Hindoo Patriot of Krishna Das Pal.

The Ilhert Bill and the change it wrought.

Then, during the viceroyalty of Lord Ripon, a revolution took place in the politics of the Indian people as the result of the violent agitation publicly conducted against the Ilbert Bill (1883) by the official Europeans who formed a pact with the non-official European trading community, lawyers, planters, and journalists and even the Eurasians. They stood up in defence of their racial privileges, as against the claim of the Indians to equality under the law and carried their point. The country was henceforth sharply divided into two hostile camps on purely racial lines. The Indians saw before their eyes an example of the strength and success of organized political agitation and of union among a community, in overawing the rulers. They had only to unite, organize themselves and follow the tactics and language of the European Defence Association and they would gain the same success.

The immediate effect of the lesson thus learnt was the assembling of the Indian National Congress in 1887. Its organizers were the orderly upper-class lawyers, to whom politics were a pleasant relaxation in the intervals of more lucrative business. Their aims and methods were far from democratic, and it was almost inevitable that they should be devoured by their children, —the middle-class democrats, at the Surat Congress of 1907. But even then, politics was still far from having been brought to the doors of the common people. That consummation was left to the period following the Great War and the initiative of Mahatma Gandhi. An appeal to the heart of the real people of India is no longer an impossibility, though their opinion, cannot be made to crystalize on a purely political issue because of their total lack of political knowledge and experience and dispersion among many provinces and castes.

The result estimated: the first faint beginnings of a nation in India.

The question will be naturally asked — What has been the fruit of this long course of political agitation by the Indians and of the gradual liberalization of the constitution by Government? When the dust of contemporary controversy is laid, when the din of our daily papers has passed into silence, it will then be found that a nation has begun to be formed in India. The people have not gained liberty, but they are now on the way to attaining that equality which is the indispensable preliminary to political liberty.

The French revolutionists fought and bled for liberty, equality and fraternity. In the end, they gained neither the first nor the third, but only the second and that enabled them to win liberty seventy years afterwards, under the Third Republic.

Liberty impossible without equality.

The *sine qua non* of democracy is absolute social equality, equal rights not only before the law but also in society, equal opportunities for all in life, and the equal reward of merit irrespective of birth, not only by the State but also by public opinion. A people with watertight class or caste distinctions, even when freed from foreign domination, cannot enjoy political liberty; it will be subject to the autocracy of a clique or a family.

Many external agencies, such as modern transport, a uniform administrative system, a common type of education, medical relief, trading and engineering works, the similarity of all our newspapers and of the method of conducting our public meetings, —all borrowed from the same western model, —are tending to standardize us, and the effect of standardization is social equality.

How the Indians are being made uniform

We already see the faint dawning of such a sense of oneness among all the Indian people. The victory of a Bengali football team over a British regiment at Simla now causes Panjabi spectators to rejoice. The sufferings of Tamil emigrants in South Africa or Fiji are keenly resented in Calcutta and Puna. There is a monotonous sameness in the agenda paper and procedure of an orthodox Hindu caste conference and say an All-India Muslim Educational Conference. Both have stolen their programme from the hated Europeans! Our nationalists denounce the West with the very arguments and methods borrowed from the West.

In addition to social equality another factor of political liberty has already been introduced in our midst, though it has not yet leavened the mass. It is self-government. The test of self-government, the true requisite of nationhood, —is not the absence of foreign dominion but the sharing by the people in the government of their own country through their representatives.

The political pre-requisites for conducting true self-government.

There has been a great deal of loose thinking and writing, many political fallacies have gained currency in our midst, because the essence of representative government has not been clearly understood. The nation's capacity for representative government is not advanced by one inch when the members of a caste in a village raise funds from among themselves and dig a public well or build a temple, or when they settle a quarrel between two caste brethren by the arbitration of five caste elders. Even when all the different castes of a village contribute to the cost of the well or temple, it is of no political value. The administration of the parish pump is no true education for the representative government of a country.

The management of parochial or communal business, —however ably or honestly done, —cannot qualify a people composed of many creeds races and provinces for conducting the State. A people have the capacity for self-government only when they can successfully administer the central government, Representative government, in its higher and only true sense, implies the power of taking a correct view of things not immediately before our eyes nor familiar to us from our childhood, the power of judging promptly and using correctly men who do not belong to our circle but come from another province or caste, in short, the capacity for using the telescope and not merely the microscope of political vision. A true nation must have an entire population of standardized normal human "spare parts", who can be fitted into every normal vacancy in the legislature or the public service, without the possibility of any difference being caused in the result by differences of race caste province language or religion among them.

Wherein modern India is relatively weaker than mediæval.

This survey of India in the modern age would be incomplete and misleading if we do not notice two points of vital importance in which we have lost ground in comparison with the Mughal period. If we cannot modernize ourselves and become capable of competing with the outer world to the fullest extent in these two respects, we are a doomed race.

Ever since the middle of the 19th century, Europe has been so rapidly and steadily advancing by the application of science to arms and to the industrial arts, that India is today much less able to wage an economic or military contest with Europe than she was in the age of Akbar. Or, in other words, our relative position has actually grown worse in the course of the last three centuries. Today, in the face of European competition, we are helplessly weak in production and exchange, and the economic drain will dry this country to death if we do not modernize our industry, arts, transport, and banking. In warfare, if India were to depend on her own indigenous resources without borrowing armament, leaders and trainers from Europe, she would not be able to stand against a modern army even for an hour. No nation can exist in the present-day world by merely cultivating its brain, without developing its economic resources and military power to the high pitch attained by its possible enemies.

The lesson of India's history.

This study of our country's history leads irresistibly to the conclusion that we must embrace the spirit of progress with a full and unquestioning faith, we must face the unpopularity of resisting the seductive cry for going back to the undiluted wisdom of our ancestors, we must avoid eternally emphasizing the peculiar heritage of the Aryan India of the far-off past. We must recognize that in the course of her evolution India has absorbed many new elements later than the Vedic Aryan age and even than the Mughal age. We must not forget that the modern Indian civilization is a composite daily growing product and not a mummy preserved in dry sand for four thousand years.

The Europeans of South Africa warned the Indian settlers there, "Westernize or leave the country." Japan learnt this secret of national preservation sixty years ago. Turkey has recently taken the hint and made her state secular and modern. To India the unmistakable message of the Time-spirit is,

"Give up your dream of isolation, standardize and come into line with the moving world outside or you will become extinct as a race through the operation of relentless economic competition in a world which has now become as one country."

LIST OF TITLES WITH ISBN NO.

ISBN	TITLE
9788194914129	1984
9789390575220	1984 & Animal Farm (2In1)
9789390575572	1984 & Animal Farm (2In1): The International Best-Selling Classics
9789390575848	35 Sonnets
9789390575329	A Clergyman's Daughter
9789390575923	A Study In Scarlet
9789390896097	A Tale Of Two Cities
9789390896837	Abide in Christ
9789390896202	Abraham Lincoln
9789390896912	Absolute Surrender
9789390896608	African American Classic Collection
9789390575305	Aldous Huxley: The Collected Works
9789390896141	An Autobiography of M. K. Gandhi
9789390575886	Animal Farm
9789390575619	Animal Farm & The Great Gatsby (2In1)
9789390575626	Animal Farm & We
9789390896158	Anna Karenina
9789390575534	Antic Hay
9789390896165	Antony & Cleopatra
9789390896172	As I Lay Dying
9789390896226	As You like it
9789390575671	At Your Command
9789390575350	Awakened Imagination
9789390575114	Be What You Wish
9789390896233	Believe In yourself
9789390896998	Best of Charles Darwin: The Origin of Species & Autobiography
9789390896684	Best Of Horror : Dracula And Frankenstein
9789390575503	Best Of Mark Twain (The Adventures of Tom Sawyer AND The Adventures of Huckleberry Finn)
9789390896769	Black History Collection
9789390575756	Brave New World, Animal Farm & 1984 (3in1)

9789390896240	Brother Karamzov
9789390575053	Bulleh Shah Poetry
9789390575725	Burmese Days
9789390896257	Bushido
9789390896066	Can't Hurt Me
9788194914112	Chanakya Neeti: With The Complete Sutras
9789390896042	Crime and Punishment
9789390575527	Crome Yellow
9789390575046	Down and Out in Paris and London
9789390896844	Dracula
9789390575442	Emersons Essays: The Complete First & Second Series (Self-Reliance & Other Essays)
9789390575749	Emma
9789390575817	Essential Tozer Collection - The Pursuit of God & The Purpose of Man
9789390896578	Fascism What It Is and How to Fight It
9789390575688	Feeling is the Secret
9789390575190	Five Lessons
9789390575954	Frankenstein
9789390575237	Franz Kafka: Collected Works
9789390575282	Franz Kafka: Short Stories
9789390575060	George Orwell Collected Works
9789390575077	George Orwell Essays
9789390575213	George Orwell Poems
9788194914150	Greatest Poetry Ever Written Vol 1
9788194914143	Greatest Poetry Ever Written Vol 1
9789390896301	Gulliver's Travel
9789390575961	Gunaho Ka Devta
9789390575893	H. P. Lovecraft Selected Stories Vol 1
9789390575978	H. P. Lovecraft Selected Stories Vol 2
9789390896059	Hamlet
9789390575022	His Last Bow: Some Reminiscences of Sherlock Holmes
9789390896134	History of Western Philosophy
9789390575121	Homage To Catalonia

9789390896219	How to develop self-confidence and Improve public Speaking
9789390896295	How to enjoy your life and your Job
9789390575633	How to own your own mind
9789390896318	How to read Human Nature
9789390896325	How to sell your way through the life
9789390896370	How to use the laws of mind
9789390896387	How to use the power of prayer
9789390896028	How to win friends & Influence People
9788194824176	How To Win Friends and Influence People
9789390896103	Humility The Beauty of Holiness
9789390896653	Imperialism the Highest Stage of Capitalism
9789390575084	In Our Time
9789390575169	In Our Time & Three Stories and Ten poems
9789390575145	James Allen: The Collected Works
9789390896189	Jesus Himself
9789390575480	Jo's Boys
9789390896394	Julius Caesar
9789390575404	Keep the Aspidistra Flying
9789390896400	Kidnapped
9789390896424	King Lear
9789390575824	Lady Susan
9789390896455	Law of Success
9789390896264	Lincoln The Unknown
9789390575565	Little Men
9789390575640	Little Women
9788194914174	Lost Horizon
9789390896462	Macbeth
9789390896929	Man Eaters of Kumaon
9789390896523	Man The Dwelling Place of God
9789390896349	Man The Dwelling Place of God
9789390575909	Mansfield Park
9788194914136	Manto Ki 25 Sarvshreshth Kahaniya
9789390896509	Marxism, Anarchism, Communism
9789390575664	Mathematical Principles of Natural Philosophy

9788194914198	Meditations
9789390575800	Mein Kampf
9789390575794	Memory How To Develop, Train, And Use It
9789390896486	Mind Power
9789390896585	Money
9789390575039	Mortal Coils
9789390575770	My Life and Work
9789390896035	Narrative of the Life of Frederick Douglass
9789390575152	Neville Goddard: The Collected Works
9789390575985	Northanger Abbey
9789390896530	Notes From Underground
9789390896547	Oliver Twist
9789390575459	On War
9789390575541	One, None and a Hundred Thousand
9789390896554	Othelo
9789390575435	Out Of This World
9789390575015	Persuasion
9789390575510	Prayer The Art Of Believing
9789390575091	Pride and Prejudice
9789390896561	Psychic Perception
9789390575381	Rabindranath Tagore - 5 Best Short Stories Vol 2
9789390575367	Rabindranath Tagore - Short Stories (Masters Collections Including The Childs Return)
9789390575374	Rabindranath Tagore 5 Best Short Stories Vol 1 (Including The Childs Return
9789390896622	Romeo & Juliet
9789390896127	Sanatana Dharma
9789390575596	Seedtime & Harvest
9789390896639	Selected Stories of Guy De Maupassant
9789390575206	Self-Reliance & Other Essays
9789390575176	Sense and Sensibility
9789390575299	Shyamchi Aai
9789390896738	Socialism Utopian and Scientific
9789390896646	Success Through a Positive Mental Attitude
9789390575428	The Adventures of Huckleberry Finn

9789390575183	The Adventures of Sherlock Holmes
9789390575343	The Adventures of Tom Sawyer
9789390896691	The Alchemy Of Happiness
9789390575862	The Art Of Public Speaking
9789390896288	The Autobiography Of Charles Darwin
9788194914181	The Best of Franz Kafka: The Metamorphosis & The Trial
9789390575008	The Call Of Cthulhu and Other Weird Tales
9789390575107	The Case-Book of Sherlock Holmes
9789390896110	The Castle Of Otranto
9789390896745	The Communist Manifesto
9789390575589	The Complete Fiction of H. P. Lovecraft
9789390575497	The Complete Works of Florence Scovel Shinn
9789390896820	The Conquest of Breard
9789390896813	The Diary of a Young Girl
9789390896332	The Diary of a Young Girl The Definitive Edition of the Worlds Most Famous Diary
9789390575701	The Great Gatsby, Animal Farm & 1984 (3In1)
9789390575312	The Greatest Works Of George Orwell (5 Books) Including 1984 & Non-Fiction
9789390575992	The Hound of Baskervilles
9789390896707	The Idiot
9789390896714	The Invisible Man
9789390575657	The Knowledge of the holy
9789390575558	The Law & the Promise
9789390896721	The Law Of Attraction
9789390896776	The Leader in you
9789390896363	The Life of Christ
9789390896196	The Man-Eating Leopard of Rudraprayag
9789390896783	The Master Key to Riches
9789390575268	The Memoirs Of Sherlock Holmes
9789390896479	The Midsummer Night's Dream
9789390575466	The Mill On The Floss
9789390896790	The Miracles of your mind
9789390896660	The Mutual Aid A Factor in Evolution
9789390896448	The Origin of Species

9789390896905	The Peter Kropotkin Anthology The Conquest of Bread & Mutual Aid A Factor of Evolution
9789390896806	The Picture of Dorian Gray
9789390896271	The Picture of Dorian Gray
9789390575275	The Power Of Awareness
9789390896356	The Power of Concentration
9788194824169	The Power of Positive Thinking
9789390575411	The Power of the Spoken Word
9788194914105	The Power Of Your Subconscious Mind
9789390896899	The Power of Your Subconscious Mind
9789390896417	The Principles of Communism
9789390575787	The Psychology Of Mans Possible Evolution
9789390896615	The Psychology of Salesmanship
9789390575732	The Pursuit of God
9789390575398	The Pursuit of Happiness
9789390896851	The Quick and Easy Way to effective Speaking
9789390575947	The Return Of Sherlock Holmes
9789390575138	The Road To Wigan Pier
9789390896981	The Root of the Righteous
9789390575855	The Science Of Being Well
9788194914167	The Science Of Getting Rich, The Science Of Being Great & The Science Of Being Well (3In1)
9789390896011	The Screwtape Letters
9789390896073	The Screwtape Letters
9789390575336	The Secret Door to Success
9789390575695	The Secret Of Imagining
9789390896868	The Secret Of Success
9789390896431	The Seven Last Words
9789390575930	The Sign of the Four
9789390896004	The Sonnets
9789390896516	The Souls of Black Folk
9789390896875	The Sound and The Fury
9789390575244	The State and Revolution
9789390896882	The Story of My Life
9789390896936	The Story Of Oriental Philosophy

9789390896752	The Strange Case of Dr. Jekyll and Mr. Hyde
9789390896943	The Tempest
9789390575916	The Valley Of Fear
9789390575879	The Wind in the willows
9789390896080	The Wind in the willows
9789390575763	Their eyes were watching gofd
9789390575831	Three Stories
9789390896950	Twelfth Night
9789390896592	Twelve Years a Slave
9789390896677	Up from Slavery
9789390896974	Value Price and Profit
9789390896967	Wake Up and Live
9789390896493	With Christ in the School of Prayer
9789390575602	Your Faith is Your Fortune
9789390575473	Your Infinite Power To Be Rich
9789390575251	Your Word is Your Wand
9789390575718	Youth
9789391316099	A Christmas Carol
9789391316105	A Doll's House
9789391316501	A Passage to India
9789391316709	A Portrait of the Artist as a Young Man
9789391316112	A Tale of Two Cities
9789391316747	A Tear and a Smile
9789391316167	Agnes Gray
9789391316174	Alice's Adventures in Wonderland
9789391316136	Anandamath
9789391316181	Anne Of Green Gables
9789391316754	Anthem
9789391316198	Around The World in 80 Days
9789391316013	As A Man Thinketh
9789391316242	Autobiography of a Yogi
9789391316266	Beyond Good and Evil
9789391316761	Bleak House
9789391316778	Chitra, a Play in One Act
9789391316310	David Copperfield

9789391316075	Demian
9789391316785	Dubliners
9789391316051	Favourite Tales from the Arabian Nights
9789391316235	Gitanjali
9789391316068	Gravity
9789391316150	Great Speeches of Abraham Lincoln
9789391316662	Guerilla Warfare
9789391316839	Kim
9789391316822	Mother
9789391316211	My Childhood
9789391316846	Nationalism
9789391316327	Oliver Twist
9789391316853	Pygmalion
9789391316334	Relativity: The Special and the General Theory
9789391316389	Scientific Healing Affirmation
9789391316341	Sons and Lovers
9789391316587	Tales from India
9789391316372	Tess of The D'Urbervilles
9789391316396	The Awakening and Selected Stories
9789391316402	The Bhagvad Gita
9789391316303	The Book of Enoch
9789391316228	The Canterville Ghost
9789391316907	The Dynamic Laws of Prosperity
9789391316006	The Great Gatsby
9789391316860	The Hungry Stones and Other Stories
9789391316433	The Idiot
9789391316440	The Importance of Being Earnest
9789391316297	The Light of Asia
9789391316914	The Madman His Parables and Poems
9789391316457	The Odyssey
9789391316921	The Picture of Dorian Gray
9789391316464	The Prince
9789391316938	The Prophet
9789391316945	The Republic
9789391316518	The Scarlet Letter

9789391316143	The Seven Laws of Teaching
9789391316525	The Story of My Experiments with Truth
9789391316532	The Tales of the Mother Goose
9789391316549	The Thirty Nine Steps
9789391316594	The Time Machine
9789391316600	The Turn of the Screw
9789391316983	The Upanishads
9789391316617	The Yellow Wallpaper
9789391316426	The Yoga Sutras of Patanjali
9789391316990	Ulysses
9789391316624	Utopia
9789391316679	Vanity Fair
9789391316020	What Is To Be Done
9789391316686	Within A Budding Grove
9789391316693	Women in Love